BUILDING A
SERVICE CULTURE

Building a Service Culture

Lifeskills International Ltd

Lifeskills team of writers:
Barrie Hopson
Jack Loughary
Steve Murgatroyd
Teresa Ripley
Mike Scally
Don Simpson

Lifeskills Series Editor: Jonathan Kitching

Gower

Published by
Gower Publishing Limited
Gower House
Croft Road
Aldershot
Hampshire GU11 3HR

Gower
Old Post Road
Brookfield
Vermont 05036
USA

Lifeskills International Ltd have asserted their rights under the Copyright, Designs and Patents Act 1988 to be identified as the proprietors of this work.

British Library Cataloguing in Publication Data
Building a service culture
    1.Customer services – Management 2.Leadership 3.Business
    planning
    I.Lifeskills International Ltd.
    658.8'12

    ISBN 0 566 08139 3

Typeset in Middlesex by SetPoint and printed in the United Kingdom at the University Press, Cambridge

CONTENTS

PREFACE

Customer service is both the oldest and the newest business issue. The earliest, most successful traders, as competition emerged, must have sought various ways to differentiate what they provided to become special in their customers' eyes. No business can survive today unless it is able to attract and retain sufficient numbers of increasingly discerning customers, and that quest will remain a preoccupation as competition becomes ever more ruthless and relentless. Astute positioning to compete on product and price can produce a short-term niche, but for most businesses the most secure route to survival and success has to come from being continually impressive and memorable to the customer through the quality of the service provided. This is a simple but powerful idea.

This book will explore the many dimensions of that simple idea and offer an approach to building service excellence that has been developed over many years through involvement in many major businesses. Over the last 20 years, as competition has reached new levels, there has been a remarkable revival of the service theme in a great many businesses. Some believed the difference would be made by training front-line, customer-contact staff to 'be nice to the customer'. In some cases millions of pounds were thrown at training programmes that quickly became known as 'smile training'. That approach, however, quickly fell into disrepute because results were short-lived. Two truths became apparent:

◆ whether or not staff smiled had much more to do with how they were managed and led than how they were trained
◆ the task was not so much to smile at the customer as to provide such an all-round quality experience for them that they would smile at you!

The learning derived from this kind of corporate experience led to the process advocated in this book. The approach recognizes that creating a consistent, quality experience for your customers, profitably, needs to be the business's real preoccupation rather than merely an internal concern for products and processes. Peter Drucker astutely reminded us that there are no results 'inside the walls': the only real result that matters in a business is a satisfied customer, and satisfaction is an outcome of getting a whole lot of things right. A quality service experience is the result of holistic, multifaceted management of many elements and will only be consistently delivered by businesses that have a deep commitment and follow a comprehensive approach. The material that follows addresses the many elements that long and extensive involvement in service-enhancement programmes suggest are the essentials.

The business case for a commitment to service is offered and then the key issue of leadership in a service business is explored; it is apparent that the pattern and style of leadership decide so much in any business. In a service business, the leadership task is to establish that a total commitment to being customer driven will be a way of life for the business, that it is the business priority and that alignment with it is mandatory not optional. If such corporate commitment is to be credible, then the next essential is that the business leadership 'walks the talk'. As Tom Peters advised business leaders, 'They watch your feet not your lips!'. People in a business claiming a commitment to quality for the customer will not be persuaded that it is a serious commitment if their leaders' behaviour suggests that it is not the real priority. Indeed, they will probably pass on to their customers the very pattern of behaviours that they experience from their managers. Without appropriate and convincing leadership, any corporate initiative will go awry. If leadership can capture the hearts and minds of those who have to deliver excellence, then the ground is fertile for establishing the service ethic.

On that ground, business success can be built by understanding the expectations of the customers you need to impress, by being clear about when and how you can be outstanding in their eyes, and by providing an all-round quality experience at every opportunity you can begin the journey to excellence. Embedding that excellence in the fabric of your business will be achieved through people development, learning from your customers, establishing standards for every part of the operation, building sound, service-based relationships between teams and functions in-house, and measuring, recognizing and rewarding high performance. It is the attention to these many factors and elements of corporate life that enables the development of a business culture that will continue to shape, ensure and maintain the delivery of service excellence over years.

This book is therefore born of experience. It is designed to be used rather than just read – and it offers a chance to build businesses that are good to work in, are prized by their customers and contribute to ever more comfortable and civilized communities in which to live.

1

WHY SERVICE MATTERS

It is becoming increasingly clear that companies are returning to an age-old business truth. This is the recognition that, in an increasingly competitive world, outstanding quality and service are essential to survival and prosperity. In the long term, external threats can only be resisted by becoming 'the customer's best choice' and by creating customer loyalty.

You probably have a sense of this already, simply because you are taking the trouble to read this book. As a manager or leader of people in a business, you are likely to recognize the importance of the 'human factor' in the delivery of quality customer service. However good your plant, your technology or even your product, it will be the performance of the people in your business that will create success. This is the power of the people in your organization to change things for the better, through their ability to shape the customer's experience and create customer loyalty.

The service age – an idea whose time has come!

We are living in an age of service. For centuries, most people in the western world worked the land. For the last 200 years we have earned our livings largely in manufacturing, making goods to sell. Now, the majority of workers are involved in service businesses, doing things that other people will pay to have done.

The service era has not arrived by accident; it is part of the evolution of society. Human beings have needs, which are great drivers or motivators. Our basic needs are for food and shelter and, if we lack these, we will strive resolutely to acquire them. If our basic needs are met, then more sophisticated ones emerge. We strive for more secure environments and more stability in our circumstances. Given this sense of physical well-being, we are still unlikely to be content. Our needs then are for acceptance and recognition, which, if we receive them, promote our sense of worth, the positive self-esteem that underpins and energizes so many facets of our lives. We want to be liked and appreciated, and respond positively to signs that we are. This is as true in the world of business and commerce as it is in our personal lives.

In the last 50 or 60 years, individuals and societies have worked through this hierarchy of needs. Most people now take for granted a relatively high standard of living. Houses, cars, holidays abroad and all manner of domestic appliances are unremarkable today. Our needs have moved beyond merely 'having'; we are in pursuit of something more sophisticated. We very much want to be treated as though we matter, we want to be valued, recognized and respected. We are hungry for the quality treatment that is a central theme of the service era.

As we shop, travel, seek entertainment, use banks, buy insurance, move house, take holidays, eat out, visit garages, take legal advice, have goods repaired, employ builders or decorators, use libraries, health services and so on, we are experiencing customer service. We are all experts on that. We know the difference between good and bad service when we see it and feel it. Businesses, including those involved in manufacturing, are having to pay very close attention to an increasingly aware and selective group of people who have the power to make or break them. The thoughts and feelings of customers have to be at the top of the agenda of any business seriously committed to success. All businesses have to be able to provide for sophisticated, discerning individuals who want more than merely the products they buy.

Obsession with the customer is the single most important factor in business success. The main priority in any business must be to win and keep the customer. Failure to do so means no profits, no growth, no jobs and no business! Success will come in our competitive world to those who recognize that:

◆ the customer is the business's biggest asset
◆ the customer pays all salaries, wages and dividends

◆ the customer will go where he or she receives the best attention
◆ in business, you must be the customer's first choice.

Those simple ideas have underpinned all great businesses in the past, and their secrets are now being sought in all corners of commerce and industry. They have become the great driving force in all ambitious companies. 'Putting the customer first' and 'making the customer boss' are now seen as the route to gaining the competitive edge.

The facts

Research shows how vital it is for businesses to retain customers, and that service quality is the one factor most likely to affect retention rates. Increasing customer retention by as little as 5 per cent can raise profits by as much as 25 to 30 per cent, and a business that can cut customer defection rates by just 5 per cent can increase the net value for each customer by 75 per cent.

In a study undertaken in association with Ventura (Customer, Ventura, Marketing Communications, 1996), the Henley Centre reveals the impact on business of poor service:

◆ In a typical medium-sized company, bad customer service can result in lost revenues of £1.8 billion over five years and lost profits of £267 million.
◆ Reducing customer service problems by a mere 1 per cent can increase profits by £16 million over five years.
◆ Eliminating all customer service problems could double profit growth over a five-year period.

Independent research commissioned by Ventura and under-taken among consumers by NOP and Principles Research (Customers, Ventura, Marketing Communications, 1997) high-lights the importance of service to customers themselves:

◆ 86 per cent of consumers expect better service than they did five years ago
◆ 82 per cent said they would switch supplier if not satisfied.

Ventura also commissioned NOP Solutions (Customer, Ventura, Marketing Communications, 1997) to carry out research among customers who had switched brands or suppliers, and discovered that:

◆ 97 per cent of multiple 'switchers' cite poor customer service as a key motivator in switching
◆ 35 per cent said that a simple apology would have prevented them moving to the competition, but nearly three-quarters of companies made no attempt to persuade these dissatisfied customers to stay
◆ customers who switch tend to be those who are the most profitable to business.

The Henley Centre has used a model to calculate the effect of poor customer service on profitability, and its findings (Ventura, Marketing Communications, 1997) illustrate the price of customer disloyalty:

◆ Reducing customer defections can boost profits by 25 to 85 per cent.
◆ The return on investment in marketing to existing customers can be three to seven times more than to prospective customers.
◆ The price of acquiring new customers can be five times greater than the cost of keeping current ones.

Feelings – a bottom-line matter!

People's feelings have not traditionally been of concern to a hard-nosed business world. However, now they are very much a bottom-line issue. Here's why.

Consider first the source of customer feelings. Every contact we make when we spend our money as a customer leaves us with an impression. Most of the time we hardly notice that impression; it is neutral. What has happened at the point of contact is unremarkable, neither awful nor special, and it has made no impact. But sometimes the way in which we are treated as a customer falls below our expectations. If we are ignored, treated rudely, somehow cheated or dealt with unfairly, then we emerge with negative feelings of anger, frustration or disappointment. We will not be keen to do business again with anyone who makes us feel like that! On other occasions, in contrast, the attention we receive as a customer seems somehow special. The person we are dealing with seems warm, friendly and attentive; he or she treats us courteously, takes some trouble on our behalf, and appears knowledgeable about the product. After such a contact we emerge feeling good about that experience, we are pleased, appreciative and no doubt ready for more of the same.

This kind of outcome is of huge significance to any business because feeling good will bring a customer back, and business success largely depends on repeat business and recommendations from existing customers to potential new customers.

The profits of loyalty

Businesses are becoming increasingly aware of the value of customer loyalty, because their success depends on repeat business and recommendations from existing customers.

If a car owner stays loyal to a particular make of car over a driving lifetime, purchasing, say, 10 new cars in that time, then that motorist can be worth anything between £40 000 and £100 000 in profit to the manufacturer and maybe half that to the dealer. If that satisfied customer is influential in convincing only one other friend or colleague about the car's worth, and thereby brings in another customer, then the value is doubled. Every contact between that customer and the business should therefore be seen from that perspective.

One disgruntled customer is a luxury that no business can afford. This is true whatever kind of business you are in. A family that spends some £30 each week at a supermarket and lives in the neighbourhood for five years will be worth around £8000 to the business in that time. If they are treated well and speak well of the supermarket to others, they can be worth many times that. Loyalty to a bank, an insurance company, a pub or restaurant, a travel agent or indeed any business adds significant benefits to that business's bottom line. So how a customer feels about, and talks about, a business translates into money and profit.

Successful businesses therefore need to be able manage the customer's feelings.

Only a little bit more

We all carry round expectations about the way things should be. We have ideas about the way we, or other people, ought to be treated, about standards of hygiene, about common courtesies, about fair play and value for money, about how long things ought to take and about many other issues. We are not usually conscious of those expectations until they are either not met or exceeded.

Bad service = when my treatment is less than my expectations.
Good service = when my treatment exceeds my expectations.

The secret of successful business lies in just exceeding what your customer expects. The old pursuit used to be customer satisfaction – it should now be that 'little bit more' that results in customer pleasure or delight! If the 'little bit more' is experienced, then customers' expectations are likely to be exceeded and they will feel that they have experienced good service. Good service can therefore be defined as 'giving customers a little more than they expect', pleasing or delighting them rather than merely satisfying them.

The features of success

There is growing recognition that only total commitment, a commitment sustained until it becomes a way of life, will deliver the consistency of quality of service demanded by increasingly discerning customers.

Governments in Europe, the US and Japan have all supported the establishment of international quality awards as a key component of improving economic performance. These awards recognize what top-performing companies have demonstrated over many years: that quality for the customer is the result of getting all the different features of a business right.

To win a national or international quality award, a company has to demonstrate all-round business excellence in areas such as the following.

◆ *Customer satisfaction.* Successful businesses know their 'critical success factors', those that keep customers loyal. They also know how customers rate the business against the competition, and this information is used to drive business performance.

◆ *People.* In such businesses, people are trained to deliver quality and outstanding service, and are also managed in a way that is consistent with the quality of treatment they give customers. This ensures that they feel part of a quality business that values people and has an ambitious commitment to continuous improvement.

◆ *Business results.* A successful business will be able to show that its investment in quality and service does indeed pay off. A key result will be the achievement of its financial targets and business objectives. Management guru Tom Peters has observed that, in his experience, those businesses that make quality and service their priority are more profitable than those that prioritize profit.

◆ *Leadership.* Excellent businesses display visible commitment to quality at the most senior levels in the organization. Leaders not only proclaim quality but practise it, through involving themselves in quality improvement programmes and taking the quality message outside the company.

◆ *Policy and strategy.* The company's values, vision and strategic direction include definite commitments to quality and service, and these are clearly translated into policies leading to successful implementation and performance.

◆ *Resources.* The management of finance, information and technology is shown to be highly effective and responsive to management, employees, customers, shareholders and the community.

◆ *Processes.* All business processes are designed to deliver quality and service to the customer, on time and profitably. The processes that lead to quality are clearly identified, owned, monitored and continuously made ever more customer responsive.

◆ *Impact on society*. Excellent businesses will be concerned for, and sensitive to, their environment. They can show that the company is perceived by the community as contributing to the quality of life, to the well-being of the environment and to responsible use of the world's resources.

Quality and service are thus products of all-round business awareness, commitment and excellence. There was perhaps a short period when customer service was thought to be deliverable through short-term training of front-line staff. Experience quickly showed that to be naive and unproductive.

What makes the difference?

Customers are a business's greatest asset. If you think that's only a cliché, you couldn't be more wrong. Customers are the one element without which a company cannot survive in a competitive marketplace. Customers now have plenty of choice; they will go where they perceive they most consistently get what pleases and impresses them.

Consider the following evidence, from worldwide research, into what makes the difference between successful businesses in a variety of fields and the rest of the competition.

Research (Buzzell and Gale, 1987) has shown that companies with a high reputation for quality service:

◆ have significantly higher customer retention rates
◆ gain a great deal from word-of-mouth advertising
◆ gain significant market share against those companies that are perceived as poor service providers
◆ have a reputation that attracts and retains talented staff
◆ have a rate of return on investment and a return on sales that are double those of companies whose service is perceived as inferior.

Your own experiences of good and bad service

It is evident that research reveals a great deal about the importance of quality service, but we hardly need research to show that it works. What about your own evidence, your own individual service experiences? How many businesses do you stay loyal to because they impress you with their care for you as a customer, and offer you quality and value on a regular basis?

Jot down three organizations that you regard as excellent providers of quality and service.

_____

_____

What, in your view, earns them that reputation?

_____

_____

Now jot down three organizations whose quality and service are unimpressive in your eyes.

_____

_____

Again, identify what it is, for you, that earns them that reputation.

_____

_____

We will look more closely at what makes the difference later.

Bad service is very costly to business. Canadian research carried out by consulting company Laventhol and Horwath, into

1000 businesses including Burger King, Procter & Gamble and IBM, showed that:

◆ poor service typically costs companies 20 per cent of their profits per annum
◆ poor service reduces sales by 10 per cent
◆ when customer service is poor, staff leave because they are disenchanted, involving significant extra expense in hiring, firing and retraining
◆ it is common for there to be a gap between top-level commitment to service quality and front-line delivery
◆ service quality suffers when there is insufficient emphasis on training and rewards
◆ poor service companies lose market share at the rate of 2 per cent per annum, while good service companies increase market share by 6 per cent per annum.

Technical Assistance Research Programmes (TARP) have researched thousands of businesses worldwide over many years, and their research shows that:

◆ 96 per cent of unhappy customers don't complain to the company whose staff displease them, but will tell an average of 10 other people about their bad experience
◆ 40 per cent of customers switching to competitors do so as a result of poor service, and 66 per cent of those do so because of a poor attitude on the part of a staff member
◆ it costs five times as much to recruit a new customer as it does to retain an existing one
◆ service companies typically lose 10 to 18 per cent of their customers each year
◆ organizations with concise, understandable and actionable service strategies and a quality service vision are four times more likely to receive superior service ratings from their customers than those without such service strategies.

The evidence is clear: excellent customer service is a key component of business success.

Enhancing the quality of service offered to customers is thus an essential requirement in today's competitive world. It is a manager's job, therefore, to lead people to believe in this imperative, to convince them to commit to it, and to be able to deliver it in their behaviour.

Your experience as a leader of people

Think about your own business and your experience as a manager or team leader. Do you believe that your own organization's quality and service are impressive or unimpressive? Why, briefly, do you think this?

What experience has your business had of gaining new customers? How are they gained?

Think of a recent occasion when your business lost a customer and jot down what happened. Why do you think this customer was lost? What could you or your organization have done differently to retain that customer?

We all know what poor service looks and feels like. Many will say that customer service is simply common sense. (Others will point out that the problem with common sense is that it's not very common!) In fact, the challenge for an organization is to take the simple ambition to be impressive to every customer, in every contact, and to build a business structure and culture that can deliver that.

References

Buzzell, Robert D. and Gale, Bradley T. (1987) *The PIMS Principles, Linking Strategy to Performance*, Free Press.

Goodman, J. and Yanovsky, M. (1997) *Enhancing the Bottom Line*, mimeo, Arlington, BA: Technical Assistance Research Programmes.

2

LEADERSHIP FOR SERVICE

This chapter explores the decisive role played by leaders in driving a service business. The crucial leadership task is communicating and demonstrating, by example and through the service delivered by leaders themselves, that the customer is the organization's primary focus. Customer-driven managers bring about continuous improvements in service standards by gaining the commitment of every member of the business to this customer focus, and by involving everyone in the standard-setting process and in the delivery of excellent service standards. Central to this process is the development of a motivating service vision that drives performance.

The material in this chapter therefore introduces a number of key concepts, such as:

◆ the nature of leadership
◆ the manager as leader
◆ assessing your own strengths as a service leader and identifying areas for development
◆ the valuable role that recognition plays in effective leadership
◆ building a customer-driven team through the creation of a service vision.

Quality leadership – a key to service excellence

Leadership is a key feature of organizations that practise service excellence. Typically, at their head will be an individual who is visibly convinced about and committed to shaping a business that is outstanding in its customers' eyes. Additionally, many service organizations now require managers to become leaders. The distinction is an important one. As change becomes ever more rapid and as competition increases, organizations need people who can lead rather than simply manage. Leadership involves inspiration, motivation, energizing others to excellence, and modelling in your own work the quality that you want others to deliver.

Let us consider more closely some aspects of management and leadership.

What is leadership?

To lead: To conduct by drawing along or preceding, or accompanying, or serving as a guide, to bring or induce by persuasion ... by supplying a motive ... by persuading or management to direct the actions or opinions of ... (Pocket Oxford Dictionary)

The word 'leadership' evokes a range of responses. What occurs to you when you think about leadership in a general sense?

_____

_____

You may have thought of political leaders such as Tony Blair, Nelson Mandela or Margaret Thatcher, or spiritual leaders like Mohammed or Mother Theresa. You may also have thought of sports leaders like Alex Ferguson, Will Carling or Sally Gunnell, or corporate leaders like Bill Gates, Anita Roddick or Richard Branson.

You may have reflected on the nature of leadership itself, for example:

◆ It is necessary in many walks of life.
◆ It is difficult to achieve anything without it.
◆ Sometimes it is bad as well as good.
◆ Not everybody is good at it.
◆ There is a shortage of good leaders.

Leadership plays a significant part in everyone's life at work, in the community, in national and local government, in churches and in social groups. In most circumstances someone is providing leadership to others.

Write down the names of two leaders you admire from any walk of life, or any era. What do you admire about them? What do you think makes them impressive?

Leader 1's name:

I admire this person as a leader because:

Leader 2's name:

I admire this person as a leader because:

Whoever you chose, you probably listed many of the qualities of leadership. On Table 2.1, tick those qualities that you mentioned or that you agree are present in good leadership.

Managers as leaders

What do you think are the main differences between a leader and a manager?

Table 2.1 *Leadership qualities*

	Tick
Strength of character	☐
Ability to communicate and influence people	☐
Credibility; easy to believe in and trust	☐
Ability to offer a vision and direction, a way to make things better	☐
Ability to accept and never shirk responsibility	☐
Ability to challenge and encourage	☐
Ability to attract and unite people	☐
Ability to get the best out of people	☐
Understanding of people and ability to make them believe in themselves	☐
Ability to get results	☐
High energy that is positively used	☐
Ability to work through and overcome difficulties	☐
Willingness to take risks to achieve success	☐

The traditional concept of a manager is someone who:

◆ controls
◆ keeps things in order
◆ keeps things as they are
◆ organizes tasks for others
◆ gives orders
◆ supervises
◆ disciplines.

However, this traditional role is not versatile enough to meet changes and new challenges, especially in businesses committed to service excellence. The need is now for leaders who:

◆ welcome change
◆ motivate others
◆ work flexibly
◆ communicate
◆ inspire others

◆ build teams
◆ meet challenges
◆ offer a clear vision and goal
◆ lead others to success
◆ are committed to service excellence for their customers.

I believe that leadership has to be endemic in organizations, the fashion not the exception! ... A leader shapes and shares a vision which gives point to the work of others.

(Charles Handy, The Age of Unreason)

Some thoughts on leadership

Table 2.2 illustrates some of the differences between managers and leaders

Table 2.2 *Differences between managers and leaders*

Managers	Leaders
Focus on doing things right	Focus on doing the right things
Focus on today/tomorrow	Focus on next month/next year
Are interested in control/status	Are interested in teamwork
Are logical/practical	Work on energy/feelings
Focus on facts/data	Can still work with what is unclear
Deliver what has been agreed	Challenge and seek new goals
Like to control people	Like people to take the initiative
Hang on to talent	Like people to get on

How would your team score you on this? Are you more of a leader than a manager in their eyes? What would it take, looking at the differences, for your to be even more of a leader in the future?

Reflect for a moment on the following questions and jot down your thoughts.

Are you currently more of a manager than a leader, and why?

Where do you exercise leadership at present?

What benefits could there be for you in developing your leadership skills?

For your business?

For others?

For your customers?

It is important to include benefits for others. Quality leaders are committed to the well-being and development of those whom they lead. Leadership requires a respect for those who are being influenced, a sense of their value and worth, a recognition that leaders can only be as good as their followers allow them to be. In service businesses, people will only pass on to their customers the quality of service that they receive from their leaders.

Everyone is a leader in some situations and a follower in others. Identify situations in which you are a follower rather than a leader, and consider the following questions.

When are you aware of being more a follower than a leader?

_____

_____

How do you feel in those situations?

_____

_____

What does that tell you about leadership? What can a leader do that will motivate or demotivate you?

_____

_____

_____

What do people say about the kind of leadership they appreciate and respond to in service organizations? Some typical comments are included in the checklist in Table 2.3. Put yourself in the place of those you work with and decide how they might describe you.

Checklist – how much of a service leader are you?

This checklist will help you focus on your service leadership strengths and identify what you can work on in the future. Tick the options that you think match the opinions of those you work with, those who know you. Be honest in your replies! What are your ticks telling you about yourself?

When you have finished, work out your score. If your score is high, then you are showing the qualities of someone who might motivate others to top service performance. Don't worry if you don't get full marks immediately; quality leaders believe in continuous improvement!

Table 2.3 *Leadership qualities checklist*

Would they say that...	Often true of you	Sometimes true of you	Never true of you
You provide a clear vision and direction that challenge and motivate your people	☐	☐	☐
You are an example of quality and service in the way you behave towards your people	☐	☐	☐
You treat your people with the same respect as you would want them to treat customers	☐	☐	☐
You lead by example – it's 'do as I do' not 'do as I say'	☐	☐	☐
You always make the customer, quality and service your priorities	☐	☐	☐
You make clear what is required to achieve success and set standards to achieve this	☐	☐	☐
You are visible; when the going gets tough you are there, leading, encouraging and supporting	☐	☐	☐
You believe in the potential of others and push and support them to achieve success	☐	☐	☐
You set challenging targets and attract a team of people who want to be the best	☐	☐	☐
You give responsibility and expect people to take it	☐	☐	☐
You communicate, informing your team, listening and responding to them and their ideas	☐	☐	☐
You are visible and available; you show interest and enthusiasm	☐	☐	☐
You work on solutions rather than complaining about problems	☐	☐	☐
People enjoy working for you; you are a good 'people manager'	☐	☐	☐
You are trusted and listened to; your people know where they stand	☐	☐	☐
You involve people because you believe that everyone has something to contribute	☐	☐	☐
You take responsibility and show loyalty to those who work with and for you	☐	☐	☐
You are consistent	☐	☐	☐
You are honest and people trust you	☐	☐	☐
You admit mistakes and work to correct them	☐	☐	☐
You are interested in results; you set clear goals and talk to your people about success	☐	☐	☐
You develop people and don't feel threatened by their progress	☐	☐	☐
You are interested in your people as individuals, not just as workers	☐	☐	☐
You believe in teamwork and stress support and cooperation	☐	☐	☐
You keep promises and don't keep moving the goalposts	☐	☐	☐
You give people space to use their initiative	☐	☐	☐
You love success; you give recognition to people for their contribution and celebrate their achievements	☐	☐	☐
Totals			

Scoring the questionnaire
Score 1 for every tick in the column 'often true of you'.
Score 0 for every tick in the column 'sometimes true of you'.
Lose 1 for every tick in the column 'never true of you'.

If your score is 22 or more, you are probably already a quality service leader, but you will not be complacent, because you will have a commitment to continuous improvement.

If your score is 16–21, you will have good potential as a potential service leader and you will be ambitious to achieve more.

If your score is 15 or below, consider the points made in the questionnaire. Pick out some key areas to work on to improve your skills in service leadership.

Enhancing your leadership skills
What thoughts did you have about your own leadership style as you were completing the questionnaire? Whatever your score, identify three things you can work on to improve it.

As you consider areas where you could develop your service leadership skills, it might also be helpful to consider some general principles of effective leadership, and the role that genuine recognition plays in building an effective team in a service business.

Leadership principles
Chinese philosophers in the seventh century BC were already establishing principles of leadership. More recent versions include the guidance that the US Marine Corps gives to its officers. This is an adapted version of those principles:

◆ *Take responsibility*. If you wish to lead, you must be prepared to take responsibility for your own actions, as well as those of the people you lead. Use your authority with judgement, tact and initiative.

◆ *Know yourself*. Be honest when you evaluate yourself and work on self-improvement.

◆ *Set an example for others to follow*. The way you conduct yourself will be more influential than instructions or commands.

◆ *Develop your people*. Set targets and goals, but give people scope for their own abilities. Match confidence in your own competence with confidence in theirs.

◆ *Be available*. Leave your team opportunities for initiative, but ensure that they know where they can find you when necessary. Stay in touch with their progress.

◆ *Be interested in people's well-being*. Respect their privacy, but be interested in them as whole people and support them when they have problems.

◆ *Keep your team members informed*. Clear, timely, regular, relevant information avoids rumour, communicates respect and builds trust.

◆ *Make prompt and sound decisions*. These will give a sense of momentum and control. If you make what turns out to be a bad decision, admit it quickly and change it.

◆ *Know your job*. Keep informed of all developments that affect your work, and be prepared to take on board new ideas if you judge them to be sound. Avoid references to the 'good old days' – there is no future in the past.

◆ *Set challenging, achievable goals*. Unrealistic targets create frustration and disappointment. People need to be stretched, but, more than that, they need to achieve success.

◆ *Build teamwork*. Show appreciation of different personalities and talents. Set team tasks and celebrate team achievements.

Which of these principles would you regard as a priority for you to focus on in pursuit of your continuous improvement as a service leader?

Leadership and recognition

The creation of an organizational climate in which service prevails is central to the service treatment that the customer receives. Staff who are treated positively will be more likely to pass on the pattern of their treatment to others and to their customers. The oxygen of a positive work climate is positive recognition of individuals for who they are and what they do.

People need recognition. Negative recognition may actually be better than no recognition at all, but what is more important for our personal well-being is *positive* recognition. We receive positive recognition when somebody praises our skills or achievements, or acknowledges our qualities. This feedback, if it is genuine, is doubly valuable: if our strengths are recognized they are reinforced. For example:

◆ tell me that you appreciate the support I give you and I am likely to give you even more
◆ tell me that the reports I write are remarkable for their clarity and conciseness, and I am likely to write even more clearly and concisely.

Each one of us likes to feel appreciated and valued. That is true for all human beings; people have a need to be somebody, to be admired and respected by others. Can you imagine anybody saying 'yes' to the question, 'Do you find you get too much appreciation?'. If the answer is 'yes', it is probably because the praise is not perceived as genuine, or the person giving it as trustworthy! Being given genuine recognition for something done well, by somebody they trust, is a motivating experience for most people.

That is a very important realization when it comes to motivating people. Giving people recognition for what they do well, for doing quality work, plays a big part in building a quality team.

'Catch people doing things right, and show appreciation for their achievement' is an excellent leadership rule. What we do when we recognize somebody's skills or abilities is to reinforce them and make it more likely that they will use those qualities again. If you tell somebody that they are really smart and look professional, you make it very likely that they will stay that way. If you tell somebody how good they are at getting on with customers, how friendly, helpful and patient they are, guess what? You're right, they are likely to be even more like that in the future.

Can you think of an example where this has happened?

_____

_____

People like working where they are appreciated. They will have more energy and enthusiasm, they will work 'beyond the contract', for leaders and organizations who praise and appreciate, rather than those who complain and criticize. Nothing succeeds like success. A quality leader sets quality targets and standards, then finds every opportunity to 'catch' people achieving these and praises their performance. This makes it clear to everybody that the way to be a winner in this team is to do a quality job.

The way you show appreciation and praise people will differ with different personalities. You will know the best approach with your own team members. Some will appreciate a quiet word of praise or a note thanking them; others will prefer to be recognized in a team situation.

Think of two or three people in your team. How could you best show your appreciation of them?

_____

_____

Think back over the last week. Was there a specific instance when you were pleased with somebody's performance in your team? How did you react? Did you show your appreciation, and, if so, how? How did the team member react?

Now take an overview of your team, asking yourself the following questions.

Are there some people who get more praise or recognition than others?

Is there more praise than criticism in your teamwork?

How would your team rate you as a giver of praise?

How can you start to build more recognition into how you manage people?

Just one word of warning: never invent praise or appreciation. People can spot insincerity and it will be counter-productive. If your attitude to your people is positive, if you really believe that they are valuable and important, then you will always see skills and qualities to admire, and in this way bring out the best in them.

In order that people are happy in their work, these three things are needed. They must be fit for it. They must not do too much of it. And they must have a sense of success in it!

(John Ruskin, 1819–1900)

Check your teamworking

You can offer the checklist in Table 2.4 to your immediate working team as a basis for analysing the quality of your teamwork. Ask people to complete it individually and then consider, as a team, suggestions for improving how you work together.

So far you have gained an idea of the skills you currently possess as a leader and have identified some areas for development. You can now turn your attention to the first stage in building a customer-driven team, and that is to create a positive customer service vision. This is as relevant to the leader of a small team as it is to the owner of a small or medium-sized business, or to a senior manager in a large corporation.

Creating a customer service vision

What is a vision?

If you don't know where you are going you may end up somewhere else.

Studies of successful service businesses have repeatedly established the significance of having a motivating, unifying business vision.

In most situations, we achieve most when we have a purpose, a vision, a mission – call it what you like – to motivate us to action. In all successful enterprises there will be a clear vision, a statement of the overriding purpose of the organization, providing a focus on which everyone can centre their efforts.

As a general rule, people will contribute more, be more motivated and work 'beyond the contract' if they are working for something they believe in and are proud to be part of. The purpose of a vision is to:

◆ provide a challenging goal to focus collective efforts
◆ provide visible evidence of a team's or organization's priorities and commitment

Table 2.4 *Team check*

So that we can make our working circumstances as positive as possible, I would value your views on the following.

On a scale of 0–10 (where 0 is low and 10 is high), how would you rate:

1 The way you are managed?

What would make this better for you?

2 The quality of communication at work?

What would make this better for you?

3 Working relationships?

What would make these better for you?

4 The support you receive to help you do a quality job?

What would make this better for you?

5 The recognition given to people for the job they do?

What would make this better for you?

6 The opportunities to develop new skills and talents?

What would make these better for you?

7 The clarity of goals and targets in your work?

What would make this better for you?

8 The quality of teamwork?

What would make this better for you?

9 The feedback on achievements?

What would make this better for you?

Thank you for your views. These will provide a good guide to future action and requirements.

◆ inspire, motivate and guide the team's efforts
◆ provide a yardstick against which to measure achievements.

The best visions can be summarized in memorable one-liners, and the goal should be 'within sight but just out of reach', challenging but achievable.

The history of the US space agency, NASA, provides one of the best examples of the motivational power of a vision. In 1960 President Kennedy provided the organization with a very clear vision:

We will put a man on the moon by the end of the decade.

The clarity of purpose and focus that this mission gave to the work of NASA produced the brightest period in its history. Its people knew why they were there, they knew where they were going, and they achieved their mission. Observers would say that it was the high point of their achievement. Since then, they have never recaptured that level of productivity or morale, because they have never been sure quite what the next mission was.

In pursuit of a similarly motivating business mission, these are the memorable ways in which some UK companies have summarized their customer service visions:

◆ 'To be the best provider of housing financial services in the UK' (a building society).
◆ 'We aim to build profitably the highest quality car in Europe' (the UK division of a Japanese car company).
◆ 'Excellence and value in meeting personal financial needs' (a major bank).

Businesses need to create a vision and embark on a process by which they gain the commitment of their staff to that vision, so that they are effective as well as efficient. An important distinction can be made between efficiency and effectiveness (see Figure 2.1).

The diagram shows six departments, each of which is efficient. However, on the left-hand side, they are all working to

Efficiency   Effectiveness

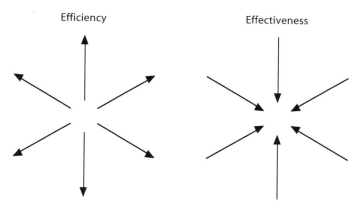

Figure 2.1 *Efficiency vs effectiveness*

different ends. The right-hand side shows what it looks like when all six departments are working to the same end.

◆ An *efficient* sales department makes many sales.
◆ An *effective* sales department makes sales consistent with production capacity and feeds back important customer information to the production, marketing and accounting departments, in pursuit of their collective purpose.

Leadership exists at all levels of an organization. Each level of leadership needs to offer a vision for those it leads. Everybody has to be clear about what is ahead, and how their role fits in with the rest of the team's. One sports club summarized this as follows:

We believe it is the director's job to look ahead to the next year. It is the manager's job to look ahead to the next match. It is the player's job to look ahead to the next move in the game.

Think about the implications of this for you and the team that you lead. Are you in the position of the director looking a year, or years, ahead, a manager looking to the medium term, or a player focusing on implementing the vision?

What is your business's overall vision?

What part do you and your team play in achieving that vision?

Creating a vision

What should an effective vision statement look like? Although, ideally, it should always be possible to encapsulate it in one line, it will initially need to be much more comprehensive. A service mission statement establishes the vision to which organizations should aspire and it speaks stirringly. For example:

- 'Service excellence is to be the beginning and end of all our efforts.'
- 'We exist only to serve our customers and in that we wish to be the best in our field.'
- 'We want our customers to have pleasure and benefit from us and our staff to take pride in being the best.'
- 'We wish to be memorable for our efficiency and customer concern.'
- 'To be profitable because we have enthusiastic and able staff dedicated to making our customers' interests and satisfaction their preoccupation.'
- 'Our customers are the most important people in our business, the ones who give us our jobs and pay our wages. Our commitment is to be outstanding in their eyes!'
- 'The customer compliments us with her attention and deserves the most courteous treatment we can give her.'
- 'We can provide the service excellence our customer deserves only through total teamwork and service to each other.'

Such statements leave no doubt in the minds of staff or customers about the nature of the task. Making the mission so public raises the stakes. It carries a high risk if delivery falls short, but its purpose is to leave no doubt as to the business priorities and expectations. It summons the troops, but it does not in itself equip them for the fray. It always states 'why' the organization exists and does not dwell on what will result – such as profit.

One major IT corporation's vision was:

To be recognized as the best provider of quality integrated information systems, networks and services to support customers world-wide.

But what does each phrase of this mission statement mean, in terms of commitment and ambition?

- ◆ 'be recognized' = we want to be the best and have our customers know it
- ◆ 'the best provider' = we are a reliable international supplier that it is easy to do business with
- ◆ 'quality' = measured by customer satisfaction and adherence to the highest standards in the industry
- ◆ 'integrated information systems and networks' = the way in which a company acquires, shares, integrates and uses data to fulfil its mission, optimize its productivity and competitiveness and plan its evolution
- ◆ 'services' = the widest range of services, from first contact through to end of product life and any services with added value to help customers design, implement and manage their information systems and networks, setting the effectiveness standard in the industry and continuing to set the pace in service technology
- ◆ 'customers world-wide' = from the individual professional to the large multinational enterprise in all its locations.

Each phrase, each word, defines the business, its purpose and its ambition.

Working on a vision for you and your team

As someone in a position to lead others, it is your job to make sure that your team has a vision – but it should not be your responsibility to create it alone. If you create a vision on your own, then you miss an opportunity to use the talents of other members of your team and to motivate them to achieve collective goals. Involving your team in creating a vision will encourage their sense of ownership – and this is a key element in motivation.

How does a team set about creating its vision? There are a variety of techniques, but to start the process, it can be useful, as a team, to:

◆ decide clearly those to whom you provide products or services (your customers)
◆ define five things that you would like your customers to say about you
◆ define five things that you would like other staff in your business to say about you
◆ define five things that you would like your competitors to say about you.

It is then possible to gain an outline for a statement of your vision. This can be done by working with your team to answer the following questions:

◆ What is the overall purpose of our work? Why does our team exist?
◆ Who are our customers, those to whom we provide products and services? What do they want, need and expect from us?
◆ Who else benefits from our work? What do we want for them?
◆ What is success for us, in the eyes of our organization, of other teams or departments, in our own eyes? What do we want people to say about our work?
◆ What will be the signs that we are achieving our vision? How will we know that we are succeeding? How will we measure our progress?
◆ When do we want to achieve these by?

From the team's answers to those questions, you can work with your team to begin to produce a concise but comprehensive vision statement, combining clarity with excitement. The outline for a statement of your vision will then need to be reworked into a clear, sharp statement that will drive and shape your team's performance. That statement can then be encapsulated in a one-liner that will be easy to remember.

Everyone in the team should be able to describe and justify the vision, and will be able to say exactly how their own work contributes to its achievement. Team members – particularly 'front-liners', those working directly with customers – are the deliverers of any customer service vision, and need to be able to answer three crucial questions:

◆ How can we contribute to this vision?
◆ How does it relate to our customers?
◆ How do we make it happen?

Each person needs their own personal vision and should know how that can fit into the larger picture.

John Harvey Jones once said:

The ideal organization, and the one with the best chance of success, is one where if you ask anyone, from the chairman down to the newest recruit on the shop floor, what the business is trying to do, you would get the same answer.

Team/business questionnaire 1 – service management

A number of questionnaires have been built into this book and can be found at the end of relevant chapters. They aim to enable you to take a look at the performance of your own business, and to score its present performance against the key characteristics of a customer-driven service business. The questionnaires are designed to help you drive improvement, as they will highlight areas where your business can build on its current strengths and areas where further development work is necessary. The exercises are of most value when a team of key players in your business can complete them. Responses are then collated to arrive at an average score for each element, as well as an overall business picture.

Table 2.5 is a service management questionnaire. The establishment of quality service standards requires management that is customer driven, leading by example through offering excellent service to staff. Customer-driven managers involve their teams in a process of continuous improvement in service standards. You now have the opportunity to score your own team or business on its customer service management.

Each statement should be scored in the following way:

Score 1: if you strongly disagree that the statement is true of your business.

Score 2: if you disagree that the statement is true of your business.

Score 3: if you see the statement as being somewhat true of your business.

Score 4: if you agree that the statement is true of your business.

Score 5: if you strongly agree that the statement is true of your business.

The scoring mechanism is the same for each questionnaire in this chapter, and in the remainder of the book.

Identify three things you, or others in your business, could do to improve your score in this area:

_____

_____

Which of these is the most important?

_____

_____

Table 2.5 *Service management questionnaire*

	Score
Management, at every level, is conscious of the special challenge of managing in a service business, the need to model excellent service in all dealings with staff, and the requirement to manage ethically and positively	
Competence in people management is at least as important as technical competence when it comes to promotion in the organization	
Managers offer strong, visible leadership, setting challenging service performance goals and motivating people to achieve them	
The quality of communication between managers and staff is very high	
Managers play a key role in the delivery of excellent service by involving their teams in a programme of continuous improvement	
We have cross-functional teams who can address service improvements that involve different parts of the business	
Managers regularly make presentations on the organization's commitment to excellent service	
Senior managers give evidence of their commitment to excellent service by their involvement in quality planning, reviewing and training	
Quality service priorities are evident in management's communications with staff and in on-going management activities	
Management has a clearly written policy statement on excellent service and a clear strategy for involving all levels in quality performance, with procedures for regular reviews	

The total possible score for service management is 50

My score for service management is	

Who will do what to achieve this?

_____

_____

Team/business questionnaire 2 – your mission or vision

Strong service businesses have strong, clear visions that make clear to people the goals they are working towards. The vision is highly visible and is used to give purpose and drive performance. The questionnaire in Table 2.6 enables you to score your business on its vision.

Three things that we could do to improve this score are:

_____

_____

Of these, the most important is:

_____

_____

Table 2.6 *Vision questionnaire*

	Score
We have a clear vision for our business	☐
The vision is challenging, inspiring and motivating for our people	☐
In our business, we recognize that service excellence is a differentiator in the marketplace	☐
Our vision drives performance in the business. People see their role and their jobs in terms of the vision	☐
Our vision is marketed internally. Business leaders continually refer to it in their contact with staff	☐
We have team/department visions that support the organization's vision	☐
Our vision is used to evaluate decisions and policies at all levels in the business	☐
The vision can be summed up as a 'one-liner', which everybody is conscious of as the ultimate purpose of the business	☐
We have visible benchmarks by which we assess progress towards achieving the vision	☐
The total possible score for vision is 50	
My score for vision is	☐

3

FOCUS ON YOUR CUSTOMERS

This chapter introduces the following key concepts in customer service:

◆ knowing your customers and understanding their expectations
◆ turning the organizational structure, or 'pyramid', upside down, to place the customer at the head of the business
◆ providing quality service to the internal customer as the basis for service quality for the external customer
◆ the customer service chain and the line manager's role within it
◆ creating a service climate.

Your company's greatest assets are your customers, but do you know who your customers really are? Do you know what they expect from you? Are you and your staff in regular contact with your customers? How do you utilize those contacts?

Two questionnaires at the end of the chapter provide an opportunity to rate your business on its:

◆ customer focus
◆ internal service quality.

'Who are your customers?' seems to be a question so simple as to be insulting to most people in business. 'Anybody who wants to buy what we provide' is the quick answer. But the skilful reply is not the quick one. There should be a measure of discernment in the successful business, identifying carefully whom it wishes to serve. Trying to be all things to all people is a business strategy with no future. Identifying market niches, attracting them, impressing them and selling to them are what business is increasingly about today.

There is good evidence of this kind of sophistication in customer focus in the modern airline industry. There is competition
among some airlines for the frequent business fliers (emphasiz-
ing the comfort of the seats and the space available on flights,
plus executive-type clubs with food and drink to ease the pain
of waiting at airports), while others focus on the customers who
want cheap, 'no-frills' flights. One airline, attempting to address
the different customer types and recognizing the complexity of
doing that, has even set up a completely separate operation to
address the cheaper end of the market. So the challenge is to be
clear just who you need to impress, and then to see your offering through their eyes, responding to, and just exceeding, their
expectations.

Of course, there can be customer segmentation within the
same business, as long as the same kind of clarity prevails.
Financial service companies, while seeking to attract and retain
prosperous client groups, also target young savers, knowing as
they do that if they can 'lock in' their customers at an early age
they are much more likely to be able to build loyalty over a lifetime. Of course, the need is to address, and market to, those different groups in a very focused way and to have a marketing
programme and products designed to appeal to their differences.

One pub and restaurant business recognized that it had to be
skilful in addressing four different customer types. It had premises in many areas of the UK, including:

◆ city centre premises catering for young people, especially at
  weekends
◆ city centre premises catering for a more sophisticated, older
  clientele
◆ country premises with an upmarket, more 'county' set of
  customers
◆ town estate premises for a less wealthy, more family-focused
  clientele.

If you think about the various circumstances that would impress
that breadth of interest, then you can begin to see the importance of having an extremely clear customer focus. As somebody

put it: 'In this kind of world, you have to throw away the machine gun and pick up the sniper's rifle.' You need clinical certainty that you are designing the customer's experience to be impressive to very diverse groups. When the hospitality business already mentioned did its customer research, it found that what made its premises attractive to the young people in city centres were the following elements:

◆ friendly bouncers (the research showed that security staff who related well to the customers, as well as maintaining the peace, were a significant asset in customer service terms)
◆ inexpensive lagers and beers dispensed quickly
◆ very loud music (conversations were a low priority) and good lighting systems
◆ trendy, modern decor.

There was no particular requirement for service staff, unless they were the source of the speedy drinks service. One researcher suggested that the ideal for these young person's pubs would be 'drink dispensers on the walls' for quick and easy access. Imagine the customers of those outlets being required to spend time in the sophisticated country hostelries, and vice versa, and you can see how crucial it is to be able to give a precise answer to the questions, 'Who are our customers?' and 'What are their expectations of us?'.

It can be useful to work with your immediate team to ensure that you have that kind of clarity, developing answers to the following questions:

In very precise terms, who are the customers, or categories of customers, to whom our business provides products and/or services? (Think in terms of age profile, income/social groupings, geography and so on.)

Looking at why those customers, or groups of customers, do business with us, what precisely do we believe that they expect from us?

What other options do customers have for acquiring the goods and services that they purchase from us? (That is, who are our competitors?)

What do we think distinguishes us from our competitors? (Why would our customers choose us?)

What, if anything, does our awareness of these issues suggest that we should do?

It is important to have clarity, but it can be presumptuous, and commercially dangerous, to believe that we can read our customers' minds. One airline went through this kind of process, with its staff responding to the question, 'What will customers expect from a world-class airline?'. The staff confidently identified that customers would want the following:

◆ modern aircraft that flew on time
◆ airports that had comfortable, attractive terminals
◆ good food and drink as they travelled
◆ speedy baggage retrieval.

In fact, when customers' expectations were actually researched, they did not mention any of the above. What was clear was that they took all these features for granted. It was as though they were saying to the airline that those things are the basics, not special, they are the 'entry tickets' to the airline business. Without them, you cannot be in the 'airline game', but they are not the factors that will make you successful in a competitive world. From a world-class airline, customers expected:

◆ individual service – they wanted to be treated as individuals, not just churned through the process as a number on a computer
◆ staff to be good problem solvers – there are frequently problems when we travel and we like matters to be put right fast! In fact, this ability to recover successfully when things go wrong is so important that the research suggested that staff and businesses who possessed it were held in higher esteem than would have been the case if nothing had gone wrong in the first place!
◆ vulnerable passengers, such as young children, the sick and the elderly, to be given special attention – this surprised researchers and staff, but customers were saying that they were sensitive to the treatment afforded to the less fortunate, and very much expected to see them particularly well cared for.

This final item was entirely unexpected and led to a review of arrangements for 'unaccompanied minors'. Because the other passengers expected to see them afforded special treatment, children travelling without adults were elevated to 'young flier' status, given games to play and a personal steward to attend to their needs. This is a good example of the importance of not guessing what the customer wants, but actually finding out, and designing services to meet those expectations. We will return to this theme.

Turning the pyramid upside down!

Part of the revolution of becoming customer driven requires a re-examination of traditional structures and of ways of thinking and working. Traditionally, organizations have looked like Figure 3.1.

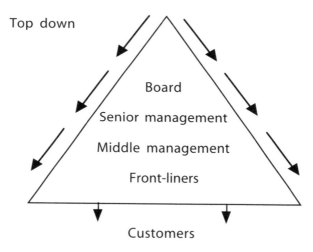

Figure 3.1 *Top-down organization*

This is a structure based on policies and decisions made 'on high', communicated down the line to low-status representatives, who deliver the product or service to the customer. The model is hierarchical, one way, formal, usually slow moving and discourages dynamism or initiative. In these top-down organizations, staff are preoccupied with what their managers want done.

In revolutionizing the organization, the message has to be that customers are more important and significant than managers. If the customer is to be 'boss', then the pyramid needs to be turned upside down, as in Figure 3.2.

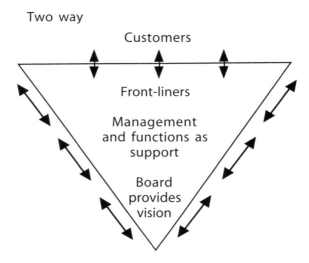

Figure 3.2 *Two-way organization*

The key players in this structure then become those who are in contact with customers, the front-liners who shape the customers' impressions of the business. For the customer, these people – the waiters, the ticket clerks, the delivery person, the counter assistants – are the company. They shape the organization's image and the customer's perceptions of it. All management, all functions, exist only to make it easier for front-liners to please the customer; any other purpose is a distraction. The pyramid in this position needs to allow continual dialogue – customer to front-liner, front-liner to management and back again. In this kind of business, staff are preoccupied with what their customers want rather than what their manager wants. The need is for drive, skill, responsibility and initiative to be shaping every customer contact, to be making it easy for customers to do business with you and helping them to enjoy doing so. The task of management is to model in their contact with staff the standards of service, the quality of treatment and the attention that they want the customer to have.

If the task of the front-liner is to be a service hero, then the role of the manager is to be a service leader.

However, there is another key realization. The quality of service that front-liners give will be decided not only by how they are managed, but also by the quality of service they themselves receive from in-house departments and functions. Consider the following examples:

◆ The financial services branch striving to provide service excellence, but finding itself frustrated by inefficiencies and lack of product development at head office.
◆ Front-line airline staff having to face irate passengers who can't fly because planes have been overbooked by the sales department.
◆ Restaurants in a chain having to waste food because it takes ages to have a fridge repaired by an under-resourced maintenance department.
◆ Front-liners in a retail outlet embarrassed because customers are expecting discounts from a sales campaign launched by head office without informing the stores.

Serving the internal customer – a basis for serving the external customer

A customer is someone to whom we provide a product or service. Everyone in an organization is therefore a customer and has customers. Even if you do not meet external customers, you will have many internal customers. You are a customer internally when you rely on other people's help and services to do your job. Your customers include other people inside the company who rely on your services to do their jobs. Other teams within the organization rely on your team to give them good service.

If staff in a business can claim:

◆ We don't support each other around here
◆ People don't seem to count in this company
◆ My manager shows no interest in what I do
◆ Things around here are very unclear
◆ I'm not sure that my boss knows what I'm good at

◆ There doesn't seem to be a lot of point in doing more than the minimum
◆ The best advice in this company is to keep your head down and your mouth shut
◆ What we are best at is buck-passing

then that business is likely to be in trouble. It needs to establish quickly whether managers act as role models to staff in providing quality service, and whether the systems are conducive to people giving good service to one another – whether, in short, there is a recognition that the quality of service that reaches the external customer begins with the quality of service that people and functions inside the company give each other.

The customer service chain

The customer service chain is the chain that links the products and services provided by your business with the customer. You, and your team, are links in that chain, whatever your job.

In any business, every job is a service job. There may be staff who say that since they never meet a customer they do not have a service job. Such statements fail to recognize the essential elements in the service network. Watch customer contact staff who are crudely managed, or do not receive the technical back-up they need, and you will see lower service standards.

Inviting staff to be preoccupied with giving the customer a positive experience carries a risk. What is good for the customer is also good for the staff. Staff who do not receive good attention themselves are likely to be cynical about offering it to others. But if every link in the chain is strong, and everyone passes excellent service on to the next link, then customers outside the organization will feel the benefit of excellent service.

Where is your team in the customer service chain?

It may be useful to work with your own team on the following exercise:

◆ On a whiteboard or flipchart, draw your version of the service chain in your business. Start with the front-liners who have contact with your external customers and work backwards, showing which departments, teams and functions provide services to those front-liners and, in turn, which departments, teams and functions support those service providers. Include all the different sectors of the business and show the service links between them.

◆ Identify who are the customers of your own team (those you provide services to) and those of whom you are a customer (those you receive services from).

◆ List them separately as either internal or external customers.

◆ If you have a range of customers, identify those whom you believe are the three key ones. In each case, specify the services that they receive from you.

Finding out from your customers

As we have established, it is most important not simply to guess what your customers want, but to find this out from them as regularly as you can. The following suggestions may be useful in helping you to do this.

Customer feedback group

It may be possible to meet a group of your customers (external or internal) from time to time and use them as a focus group, a source of feedback. In such sessions, the task is to make them feel welcome and comfortable, telling them that you would like their help to make your products or services even better for them. Ask them to tell you:

◆ the three most important things about the service they receive from you

◆ how well they think you are doing in providing what they want at the moment

◆ what they think you do well as a team or as a business

◆ how, in their eyes, you could do better.

Point out that while it is not always possible to provide everything they want, if it is within the power of your team or busi-

ness to meet their expectations, you will work towards doing so.
Thank them for their help. Generally, customers are impressed
when they are asked for their ideas.

A customer survey

Rather than meeting a group of customers, it may be better to
offer a larger group the chance to tell you their ideas through a
simple customer survey. It can be useful to hand a survey similar
to the one in Table 3.1 (used in a retail business) to a representative sample of customers, or to make it available in the areas
in which you meet your customers.

For internal customers, the research options are actually very
similar. Table 3.2 is a survey form used between departments in
one operation. Ratings are 1–5, where 5 is high.

It can help to get specific customer comment not just on
service performance, but also on what, in their eyes, represents best practice in the pattern of service they receive. Table
3.3 is an example of one department's method of gathering
that data.

Analyse the views that come back to you. Recognize the real
messages and, as a team, discuss what you can do to be even
more impressive to the customers that you serve.

Service promises and guarantees

When you are clear about the expectations of your external customers, and when you have ensured that your people have the
capacity to deliver your products and services consistently to
these standards, then you can decide to 'go public' with the
standards you will promise, or guarantee, to your customers. If
these can be delivered, then this kind of confidence can be
impressive and attractive to customers. If, however, the ability
to deliver against these consistently is in any doubt, then it
would be wise not to go so public. The soundest advice to service providers is, of course, to 'under-promise and over-deliver'
rather than vice versa. There is nothing quite so embarrassing or
commercially damaging as going public with rash promises that
then remain undelivered.

Table 3.1 *Customer survey*

Our service rating

We would like your help in rating the quality and service that we provide for you. We want to offer all our customers excellent standards and, to do this, we need feedback on our performance. Please give us your views.

	Yes	No
Product and presentation		
Were our premises clean and attractive?	☐	☐
Were our displays neat and tidy?	☐	☐
Were all floors and surfaces clean and free of dust and litter?	☐	☐
Were the aisles clear of boxes and packaging?	☐	☐
Were the displays appropriately full?	☐	☐
Were the areas you visited clean, tidy and pleasant smelling?	☐	☐
Was the till area neat, tidy and well presented?	☐	☐
Procedures		
Were opening hours clearly visible?	☐	☐
Were size and price tags easily identifiable?	☐	☐
Were graphics displaying new or sale items visible?	☐	☐
Were staff easily identifiable and wearing badges?	☐	☐
Was the refund policy explained?	☐	☐
Was the till point sufficiently staffed for the number of customers waiting?	☐	☐
Were there three or fewer customers waiting in the queue?	☐	☐
Did you feel that the queue was efficiently managed?	☐	☐
Was your transaction handled smoothly?	☐	☐
Was your change counted back to you?	☐	☐
Were purchases packed properly?	☐	☐
Was the receipt placed in the bag?	☐	☐
Was the bag handed to you?	☐	☐
Was there an obvious management presence?	☐	☐
Did you feel that the establishment was well/smoothly run?	☐	☐
People		
Were you acknowledged by a staff member on arrival?	☐	☐
If yes, was it within 30 seconds?	☐	☐
As you browsed, were you acknowledged by staff?	☐	☐
When you were in contact with staff, were they friendly and helpful?	☐	☐
Were you approached when you looked as if you needed help?	☐	☐
Were questions answered quickly and knowledgeably?	☐	☐
Did the assistant seem enthusiastic about the products?	☐	☐
Did the assistant ask questions to understand your requirements?	☐	☐
Were complementary/accessory products recommended?	☐	☐
If the product you wanted was unavailable, were efforts made to help you?	☐	☐
Were you encouraged to try the products?	☐	☐
Was there a member of staff on hand to help if required?	☐	☐
Were you acknowledged on arrival at the till?	☐	☐
Were you dealt with in a polite and friendly manner?	☐	☐
Do you feel that your custom was valued?	☐	☐
Were you thanked for your custom and bid a friendly farewell?	☐	☐

Table 3.2 *Internal customer survey*

Departmental research

From... To..

In pursuit of excellence in all aspects of our work, we would appreciate your rating of our department's performance over the last month. Thank you for your help in our programme of continuous improvement.

Products or services received from us

Your rating

Comments on the rating (if any)

Our procedures

Your rating

Comments on the rating (if any)

The staff who dealt with you

Your rating

Comments on the rating (if any)

Internal service contracts

Having clarified what the expectations of internal customers are, and having geared up as a team to deliver these consistently, then it is possible to formalize them into internal 'service contracts' (or promises), in which departments agree the standards of service that they will deliver to each other in a particular period. Surveys can be carried out regularly to ensure that each

partner in the contract is satisfied with the delivery, and programmes of recognition and reward can be established to recognize achievements in those areas.

Table 3.3 *Best departments*

> In our opinion, the best ....
> departments:
>
> DO ....
>
> DO ....
>
> DO ....
>
> In our opinion, the best ....
> departments:
>
> DON'T...
>
> DON'T...
>
> DON'T...
>
> From:...

What will your team say to those people who provide services
to them about standards of excellence in the future?

What will your team members promise to those they serve in
terms of standards of service in the future?

Think about the work of your own team, and list four ways in
which your team members can offer even better service and
support to each other.

If all the people in your list and in your team work together even more effectively, what will be the benefits for:

You?

Your colleagues?

Your customers?

Your business?

It is extremely important that everybody in the organization understands the 'service network' inside the organization, and their part in it. Everybody has a customer and everybody is a customer. There must be as much readiness to offer quality and service to customers inside the organization as there is to external customers. In progressive service companies there will be standards and service contracts agreed between functions and departments inside the business, as a basis for producing the quality required externally.

Your role as manager or team leader

Typically, promotion to team leader or manager has been given to those who were more technically skilled than their peers. Often, too late, many realized that technical skills do not necessarily equip one for people management.

Line managers, in their role as team leaders, are key players in creating and leading a quality service culture. One theory suggests that 85 per cent of what happens in business comes down to management, so any initiative that fails to recognize its importance is likely to sink without trace. Line managers and team leaders must have the skills of leading and sustaining a service revolution. Below are some other competencies that effective service managers are likely to have:

◆ *people skills* – the ability to listen, show understanding, be courteous, give time, encourage, support and give recognition to the people they manage
◆ *passion* – the ability to enthuse, excite and present a vision that will motivate
◆ *leadership qualities* – a real belief in people's ability to transcend the ordinary, which translates into delegation and empowerment.

Leadership means achieving through people, offering clear goals, encouraging participation, involvement and creativity. It means setting standards, measuring progress, making success visible. It means making feedback constructive and requiring people to learn from mistakes. It means making clear 'what' is to be achieved, but leaving the 'how' to your people, trusting them, making them responsible. It means creating a service climate.

Creating a service climate

What does it feel like to walk into a reception area and see staff bang things down on the desk in front of one another? Or visit a restaurant where the waiters are clearly at odds with one another and with the chef? These patterns are indicators of their organization's 'climate'. Creating a good service climate does not only make day-to-day life for staff more pleasant, but there is a 'knock-on' effect on the customer.

Human beings pass on the kind of treatment they receive.

If we are treated positively ourselves, we are much more likely to treat others positively. This is a key piece of awareness for service teams. Service providers must model the treatment they want for the customer in their dealings with each other. Service must exist inside an organization before it can be exported, and a positive, encouraging, supportive and confident climate is the basis for it.

The most significant element in creating a positive work climate will be your personal behaviour as team leader, but such a climate is not only built by interpersonal contacts. The organization can assist the process a great deal by providing a creative and exciting environment. The work environment is a shaper of attitudes and behaviour, so an investment in it is an investment in service performance.

Table 3.4 includes some other ideas for creating a positive work climate. Tick those that might work in your own situation, and plan to introduce them gradually so that they become a natural part of your teamworking.

Create excitement and stimulate interest in a host of ways. Tap into people's positive, creative spirit so that energy is always used positively and they are drawn into that style of culture!

Team/business questionnaire 3 – focus on your customers

The questionnaire in Table 3.5 focuses on a further area that has been shown to be significant in organizations that are establishing a quality service business. The scoring system provides a method of identifying strengths and development needs. The process should lead to discussion, priorities and an agenda for action.

Service businesses display an obsession with the customer. You now have the opportunity to score your own business on its

Table 3.4 *Creating a positive climate*

	Tick
Design events that give a positive start to each month, each year, to new projects and new phases of projects	☐
Make a positive start to days and weeks and to meetings – it may only be a matter of coffee, cakes, kind words and helpful ideas	☐
Have positive, encouraging notices or posters in your team's work area	☐
Make the work area beautiful – attractive settings lift people, whereas ugliness depresses. Have light rooms, pleasant colours, comfortable chairs and cheerful pictures	☐
Ask your team to draw up a list of '10 ways to improve our environment' and get them to implement the best ideas	☐
Have plenty of plants and trees around – these have a very positive psychological effect	☐
Give people the option of having occasional pleasant, inspiring music as a background to work	☐
Display photographs of your team and key customers, rather than just names, to help make people more real to each other	☐
If your workspace has a reception area, have an excellent receptionist to make that all-important first impression positive. Ensure that he/she is a model, not a substitute, for everybody else being welcoming	☐
Have special events for staff – theme days, trips out, special exhibitions, sports events, social outings, treasure hunts, music or cultural events, wine tasting etc.	☐
Display your best products, or features of them, in your work area	☐
Insist that all team energy is used positively – have a 'no moans, no gripes' contract	☐
Encourage attractive clothes and appearance – high standards promote self-esteem and convey respect for colleagues and customers	☐
Encourage and reward stylish ways of working and delivering products and services to your customers – 'It's not just what we do but the way that we do it!'	☐
Go public with your vision when the time is ripe, so that your people and your customers know of your aspirations and ambitions	☐
Ban the phrase 'Yes, but...', which is the introduction to so many negative responses. Recognize and reinforce the response 'Yes, and...'. Challenge your people to adapt and build on ideas rather than rejecting them	☐
Make every job as interesting as it can be – ask the person who does the job regularly, 'How can what you do be made more interesting for you?'. Always ensure that people have challenge and achievement in their jobs	☐

Table 3.4 *Creating a positive climate (cont.)*

Give people recognition for the job they do and reward them well ☐

Produce posters of what you want your customers and colleagues to say about the work of your team; challenge your team always to work to achieve that reputation ☐

Remember special details about people in your team – their birthdays, their children's names, their favourite colours, foods and music, their hobbies, special talents and skills – and find occasions to show that these are remembered ☐

Have a team contract that everyone has to perform one five-minute act of very special service to other team members every day ☐

Celebrate as a team – birthdays, anniversaries, spring, summer, autumn, winter, the start of public holidays, new ideas, new projects, new contracts, customer compliments, and anything else that recognizes people and their successes ☐

Support everybody as a way of life, but rally round those who carry heavy burdens and are under pressure at particular times ☐

Seek out any quality shortfalls or complaints, internal or external, seek fast, effective recoveries, and challenge your team with the question, 'What can we learn from that and how do we avoid a recurrence?' ☐

Provide treats when they are least expected, or even least deserved! Chocolates, cakes, a glass of wine, a cup of special coffee, a long lunch break, a bunch of flowers and thank-you cards all register for people that they are the key to success ☐

Share out the more boring and mundane work, as well as the opportunities to do what is interesting and creative. Get others involved whenever anyone has an especially demanding task ☐

Develop a '10 ways to . . .' pattern of thinking for your team – ask them to produce 10 suggestions for making customers welcome, celebrating achievements, having more fun, improving teamwork, offering even better customer service, or whatever else will make your team special. Produce copies of the ideas for team members and encourage them to use them. Every six months, have a 'creative party' with the challenge to introduce new ideas 'to make us even more successful in the future' ☐

Spend quality time with each other and organize happenings outside work ☐

Recruit positive, confident, energetic people, and support them at every opportunity. Use your best people to train new recruits ☐

customer focus. The exercise is most valuable if a team of key players in your business can complete the questionnaire, and then discuss their views as a team.

Each statement should be scored in the following way:

Score 1: if you strongly disagree that the statement is true of your business.

Score 2: if you disagree that the statement is true of your business.

Score 3: if you see the statement as being somewhat true of your business.

Score 4: if you agree that the statement is true of your business.

Score 5: if you strongly agree that the statement is true of your business.

Three things that we could do to improve this score are:

Of these, the most important is:

Team/business questionnaire 4 – internal service quality

Customer-driven businesses are clear about the importance of internal service and its impact on the external customer, and teams within them understand their position in the customer service chain. You now have the opportunity to score your own team on its internal service quality. The exercise is most valuable if all team members can complete the questionnaire in Table 3.5.

Table 3.5 *Customers questionnaire*

	Score
We have a very clear profile of the customers that our business needs to attract	☐
We know exactly what those customers want and expect of us, and are committed to providing this	☐
We have a range of strategies for learning from customers and measuring their level of satisfaction with performance	☐
The data we collect from customers is used as a basis for management policies and decisions and in the design of products and services	☐
We use data from customers in our training of front-liners	☐
Our priorities are those given to us by our customers	☐
We guarantee customers standards of service excellence and measure performance against those standards	☐
Everybody in the business recognizes that the customer pays all wages and salaries, creates all profits and provides all jobs, and is the most significant person in the company	☐
Everybody knows the potential value of a typical customer who stays loyal to the company	☐
Everybody knows what our business performance is in terms of customer retention	☐

The total possible score for customer focus is 50

My score for customer focus is	☐

Table 3.6 *Internal service questionnaire*

	Score
Everybody is clear who they provide service to (their customers) and who they receive service from	
Standards of performance are agreed for internal service between teams and departments and regularly reviewed	
People and departments have the resources to meet the reasonable expectations of their internal customers	
People and departments respond quickly and effectively to the unforeseen needs of their internal customers	
People and departments are flexible when circumstances require deviation from policy to meet the reasonable needs of internal customers	
We have high-quality communication between internal customers. There are no surprises when there are delays or problems	
People and departments are held accountable for their service commitments to internal customers	
There are high levels of understanding and trust between people and departments within the business	
The total possible score for internal service quality is 50	
My score for internal service quality is	

Three things that we could do to improve this score are:

Of these, the most important is:

4

CREATING YOUR CUSTOMER'S EXPERIENCE

This chapter offers an insight into three key customer service ideas:

◆ moments of truth – the significance of each contact made with a customer
◆ managing the customer's experience – 'the 4 Ps' of people skills, product, presentation and processes
◆ keeping customers satisfied and loyal.

You are invited to score your own team or organization by completing two questionnaires at the end of the chapter:

◆ the 4 Ps
◆ moments of truth.

In business, you are never simply providing a customer with a product or service. You are in fact creating an experience for the customer around the product or service – hopefully a positive experience, but sometimes it can be negative. The quest, in the ambitious business or team, is to make every customer contact special or memorable because it leaves a positive impression.

A customer's experience is made positive or negative by the gap between their treatment at the point of contact and their expectations.

We don't know what good service is ... until we don't get it!

We all carry around expectations of which we are not conscious until they are not met. We expect courteous treatment, value for money, promises to be kept and so on. Our treatment as a customer can produce one of three outcomes:

◆ When our treatment exceeds our expectations, the result is pleasure or delight and the outcome is positive and memorable.
◆ When what happens is exactly what we expect, the result is neutral, unremarkable, run-of-the-mill.
◆ When our treatment is below expectations, then the outcome is disappointment, frustration, even anger.

Good service is giving the customers a little more than they expect.

The secret of business is to just exceed what your customer expects. The old pursuit used to be customer satisfaction – it now needs to be 'that little bit more' that results in customer pleasure or delight!

Can businesses give more and still survive? Giving people a little bit more than they expect is a simple idea, but one that involves great subtlety. Consider the following cases.

◆ A couple dine out in a restaurant. They are made very welcome and the food is excellent and served stylishly. After paying the bill, they are helped on with their coats and, as they are leaving, the woman is presented with a beautiful red rose in memory of the visit.
◆ A businesswoman visits a hotel. She knows to expect a friendly reception, efficient check-in procedures, a well-decorated room, a comfortable bed, a telephone and television that work, and a clean bathroom with sufficient towels. What she does not expect is to find a handwritten note from the manager welcoming her, wishing her a pleasant stay and giving her his telephone number to use in the event of any problems.
◆ A man purchases an oven from a local retailer. A few days later he receives a note from the store thanking him for his custom, inviting him to telephone if he is experiencing any difficulties, and enclosing a complimentary cookbook.

Most customers' reactions to such touches are very positive. They are thoughtful, even elegant, gestures that round off an already satisfactory, or even enjoyable, experience. It is interesting to reflect, however, on what might have been the reaction of the first customer if she had been handed a bouquet of two dozen roses. Most people would feel uneasy or suspicious, because the gift would seem too generous. Perhaps some would be inclined to look at the bill again or believe that they had been charged too much in the first place. In other words, giving people a lot more than they expect is likely to put them off or make them wary. It will also increase the costs of doing business to the extent that the business itself may be jeopardized!

Good service is cost effective. The secret is to be excellent in many things that don't cost money as well as in things that do.

Remember, it is only service that is out of the ordinary that becomes memorable. The business task is to make every contact memorable because it is impressive.

If customers are now more discerning and sophisticated, then those who serve them have to be the same. The immediate need is to be able to 'read' your customers' expectations, and to look at your business, and their moments of contact with it – moments of truth – through their eyes. Quality service is in the eye of its recipient!

Moments of truth

When do we make the decision that:

◆ a hotel is really good?
◆ a shop or bank is worth doing business with?
◆ we will return to a restaurant?
◆ we will fly with an airline again?
◆ we will take our car back to a particular garage?

These decisions are not likely to be made as a result of long, careful analysis. Rather, they will be a direct result of our experiences of the business or its products, an experience built up of brief encounters with a range of features that could be described as 'packaging' around the core product or service. These brief encounters between a customer and a staff member may only last a few seconds, yet each of these moments of truth contains the potential for the customer to experience feelings ranging from magical to nightmarish, passing through all points on the journey, including indifference.

The phrase 'moments of truth' comes from the world of bull-fighting and the *corrida*. It is that moment towards the end of the fight when the matador and the bull face each other eye to eye. Each of them has an instant to make a decision, and the outcome of the event is determined at that moment. Describing every point of contact in a service context as a 'moment of truth' establishes just how significant and decisive is every point of contact with the customer.

As one airline's chief executive officer put it:

SAS has 10 million passengers a year. The average passenger comes in contact with five SAS employees. Therefore SAS is the product of the 10 million times the five. SAS is 50 million moments of truth per year. Fifty million unique, never to be repeated opportunities to distinguish ourselves in a memorable fashion, from each and every one of our competitors.

(John Carlzon, CEO, SAS)

Reflect on your own business. It will contain many thousands of moments of truth between you and your customers. How you measure up at these moments will determine whether that customer with whom you make contact:

◆ becomes your customer
◆ remains your customer
◆ brings new customers to you by spreading the good news.

Impressing customers in a non-retail environment can be more challenging, but again it will call for a study of where, when and how you affect your customer so that you become impressive and memorable, and for effective management of those circumstances. For example:

◆ In direct financial services, the customer is highly influenced by the warmth and friendliness in the voice of the person they talk to but never see, by the simplicity and user-friendliness of the procedures they are led through and, of course, by the accuracy and security of any transaction.

◆ In Internet-based businesses, the customer will be impressed by the creativity of the Website, by the speed of any response to information requested, by the timely and safe delivery of any goods ordered, by the support services provided and by the quality of the on-going contacts.

◆ In the provision of home-based entertainment and communication cable services, customer opinion is shaped by the range and quality of the services, but also by the speed and reliability of the back-up provided when things go wrong.

◆ In the provision of legal or house-purchase services, there will inevitably be significant customer interest in the charges to be made but, beyond those, impressions will be shaped by how much stress the provider can take out of the process, how much they 'take the strain', take the initiative and deliver on their promises.

Whatever business you are in, the task is to be clear about any opportunities that you have to have an impact on the customer, about their expectations in those circumstances, and about what you might do to suggest that the business provides 'that little bit more'. This is what makes customers feel special and separates, in their minds, the best businesses from the rest.

So how does your business measure up? Are customers impressed by each contact they make? You can analyse the moments of truth in your organization by putting yourself in the customer's shoes and examining the contact from their point of view. Remember that no one moment is more important than the customer's first contact with a person.

Complete the checklist in Table 4.1 and note your impressions. Which are the moments of truth? Which are impressive or less than impressive? Put a tick in the appropriate box

Table 4.1 *Moments of truth checklist*

	Good	Neutral	Poor
First impressions – entrance (visual impression)/ first contact (non-visual impression)	☐	☐	☐
Selection of services/products	☐	☐	☐
Quality of services/products	☐	☐	☐
Layout of premises/user-friendliness of processes	☐	☐	☐
Cleanliness of premises/simplicity of processes	☐	☐	☐
Staff greeting	☐	☐	☐
Availability of staff	☐	☐	☐
Physical appearance/professionalism of staff	☐	☐	☐
Availability of information	☐	☐	☐
Staff response to a request or query	☐	☐	☐
Friendliness of staff	☐	☐	☐
Way staff say goodbye	☐	☐	☐
Overall impression	☐	☐	☐

according to whether you think each element is good, neutral or poor. Ask the following questions in relation to each element:

◆ What does the customer want and expect?
◆ Are we providing that *and* a little bit more?

If you go through the checklist and examine those moments of truth that you have assessed as neutral or poor from the customer's viewpoint, you will probably be conscious of what it would take to make them impressive.

Make a list of the things that you could do to make the most of your moments of truth, and decide which improvements can be made in the short term and which will take longer.

Improvements that we could make straight away:

Things that we need to work on in the longer term:

Any more?

A preoccupation with moments of truth is the key to service success. Quality service, however, requires more than mechanically good service at moments of truth. If good service is giving customers a little more than they expect, then excellent service involves enthusiasm and enjoyment in doing so. The definition can be expanded to read:

Excellent service = enjoying giving people a little more than they expect.

The best service companies have a passion for service excellence – providers of service excellence do it with energy and enthusiasm!

Excellent service is very much a 'win/win/win' experience:

◆ The customer obviously wins through being on the receiving end of quality provision and attention.

◆ The service provider wins because the customer's pleasure and satisfaction are reciprocated. The provider has the satisfaction of a job well done. Self-esteem and confidence are built by quality job performance.
◆ The business wins because the quality of the service experience brings the customer back to buy again and, because most people talk about such experiences, they become living, walking advertisements that draw other people to the business.

A moment of truth has been well managed when the customer walks away feeling enriched and delighted by the experience.

Managing the customer's experience – the '4 Ps'

When we use a service or buy a product, we are not usually aware that our experience as a customer is being managed. This is at it should be, because the best customer service should feel natural and not staged. On the other hand, how often have you experienced the opposite – not that you are being managed, but that no one cares a hoot what your experience is, or what images you take away?

As businesses grow, it is easy for them to lose sight of the basics. People can become distracted by the complexities of building the business and managing increasingly large numbers of staff. If this happens, they can easily lose sight of the simple, essential purpose of any business, which is to satisfy and retain the customer. Quality service companies have staff who always see their key purpose as impressing the customer, who realize that all else is secondary. They see their job as never just to sell a product or service, but rather to delight or impress their customer as they do so.

Any customer's experience of a business is decided by the '4 Ps', a method for analysing the components of the customer's experience:

◆ *People skills* – the quality of the interaction that they have with those providing the service.

◆ *Product* – the quality of any goods that they purchase.
◆ *Presentation* – the impression created by the 'wraparound' to the product or service (premises, paperwork, packaging and so on).
◆ *Processes* – the efficiency and 'customer-friendliness' of the systems and procedures that allow the customer to receive products and services quickly and smoothly.

To achieve service success, you need to manage the customer's experience of your business by ensuring that:

◆ all your staff have excellent people skills
◆ you are selling or offering superb products
◆ your presentation of the product or service and its surroundings is excellent
◆ the processes delivering or supporting the product or service are customer centred.

The first P – people skills

The success of a service business depends on the people who staff it. Customers will be turned on or off by the people, so there is a need to invest in people skills. Customer-contact staff require six main abilities:

◆ to make people feel special
◆ to manage first and last impressions
◆ to maintain a positive attitude
◆ to communicate clear messages
◆ to show high energy
◆ to work well under pressure.

You can use the following mnemonic to help you remember these six skills:

The customer comes 1st:

C = *clear messages*
O = OK *attitude*

M = *making people feel special*
E = *energy*
S = *service under pressure*
1st = *first and last impressions.*

Let's look at each of the six people skills in turn.

Making people feel special

Human beings love quality treatment. We love to feel wanted, valued and respected. We find such treatment irresistible; the need for it is built into us. Any business recognizing and delivering this is on to a winner. The basis for all quality contact is real respect, demonstrated in behaviour. For example, we feel special when people:

◆ listen to us and respond to what we say
◆ go to some trouble to provide what we need
◆ give us time and quality attention
◆ use our name when appropriate
◆ are courteous, polite and welcoming
◆ show interest in our ideas and experiences and ask questions to find out what we think and how we feel
◆ make us feel comfortable and solve our problems
◆ provide that little bit more than we expect.

Part of making people feel special is recognizing their uniqueness. Each of us is a mixture of genes, personality and experience that makes us a one-off. What excites one person may bore another. What one regards as valuable will be unimportant to another. We can make generalizations about what people have in common, but we must not lose sight of the fact that each of us is unique and different.

At moments of truth, we need to recognize that the customer's world and experience are different from our own. At this point, what customers want is for us to understand them, to put ourselves in their place and see their point of view. The best service providers show understanding, they empathize, they put themselves in the customer's shoes. They look at a situation through the customer's eyes. We are likely to feel understood when:

◆ people pick up not just what we say but also how we feel
◆ they show in their faces that they are on our wavelength – concerned if we are not, amused if we are – and they respond accordingly
◆ they don't allow their views to deny our experience, but accept what we say
◆ they adjust their views on the basis of what we say.

In quality service situations the customer always feels understood, and feels that the provider is seeing things from their point of view.

A further key area of people skills is the ability to inspire trust. In situations of quality service, the customer does not feel manipulated or controlled, but experiences the provider as genuine, trustworthy and reliable. Trust does not just materialize. It has to be built and maintained; it is a keystone of excellent service.

People show they are genuine and can be trusted when:

◆ they are open and honest about themselves and about their products and services
◆ they take responsibility
◆ they admit mistakes and shortcomings where they exist
◆ they keep promises
◆ they follow through and show that they are reliable
◆ they are consistent
◆ they put themselves out to help others
◆ what you see is what you get!

Excellent service always conveys and promotes trust by conveying the genuineness of the provider.

When it is communicated at moments of truth that the customer is respected and understood and they are treated genuinely, the foundations are laid for quality customer service and long-term loyalty.

First and last impressions

A high level of people skills will make a positive customer experience likely. However, the biggest threat is lack of time. When we are rushed or under pressure, our best intentions are most at risk. The temptation may be to rush all we have to do because there is more waiting to be done. Dealing with customers at such a time requires a steady hand, because lasting impressions are built from first impressions.

Research suggests that the opening minutes of any business contact are of great importance. In those opening few minutes, many impressions are created and conclusions drawn. Each of us will rapidly assess how important we are to the other person and how much the other cares, is interested, concerned, enthusiastic, willing to help or otherwise. It is as if we give each other the first few minutes as an opportunity. After that we make up our mind about people. If we are dealing with a customer in that time and we are officious, impatient, impersonal or inattentive, then recovery will be difficult. If we are pleasant, courteous and responsive, we will have established a solid foundation.

It is not just first impressions that are crucial, however. We need to give as much thought to what we do as customers leave us as we do to when they first make contact.

The last impression lingers longest.

How can we make the most of the first and last contacts? We can:

◆ avoid ritual or routine activity or standard phrases
◆ smile – even when we answer the telephone, the other person can hear it
◆ avoid moans, groans and negative comments, about ourselves, work or other people – even about the weather!
◆ treat customers as special, making every customer our favourite
◆ avoid rushing or doing too many things at once
◆ find out the customer's name as soon as possible, and use it
◆ look at customers, take an interest in them and pay attention to how they are, and what they are doing and saying

- avoid chatting to other staff when customers are around
- greet them with enthusiasm and look for positive, genuine things to say about them
- assess what kind of help they want. Do they want to be left alone? To be approached? To be chatted to?
- have something positive to say when the customer leaves
- get a definite closure and not just let contacts ebb away.

When you're serving a customer, you're on stage. Are you dressed for the part? Do you know your lines? Do you understand the play?

An OK attitude

When reporting dissatisfaction with the quality of service they receive, customers frequently observe that the problem comes down to 'staff attitude'. The attitudes adopted by the service givers to themselves and to their customers are the service launchpad. Attitudes shape behaviours and responses. Awareness of our basic attitudes helps greatly in service situations.

The transactional analysis model of human behaviour provides us with a shorthand way of understanding what happens between people. We each have basic attitudes to ourselves and to other people. In terms of a view of ourselves, we can be anywhere on the continuum:

I'm OK . . . . I'm not OK

A person with an 'I'm OK' attitude sees herself positively. She is aware of her skills and qualities, her value as an individual, and she has basic confidence in herself. People operating from this position have no illusions about perfection. They are aware of shortcomings and potential in themselves, but see those as areas to work on, rather than reasons to doubt themselves or their ability.

Someone whose basic attitude is 'I'm not OK' lives with self-doubt and self-criticism. His experience is consistently negative, focusing on faults and failings, seeing little value in himself and viewing all contributions that he might make to situations as largely futile.

As well as attitudes towards ourselves, we subconsciously carry around attitudes towards other people. These attitudes can also be seen on a continuum:

You're OK . . . . You're not OK

A person whose basic attitude to others is 'You're OK' sees other people as worthwhile, significant and of value. She will see their talents and qualities and will be aware of their skills and contribution to any transaction.

On the other hand, some people see others as basically 'not OK'. This attitude causes them to view people as not worthwhile. They will be aware of others as nuisances, as problems, as irritants, seeing inadequacies and failings in others before seeing anything else.

A great deal of what happens between people can be explained by piecing together these attitudes towards ourselves and others. The continua combine to give us four quadrants (Figure 4.1).

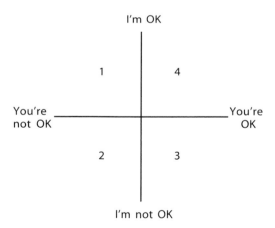

Figure 4.1 *I'm OK, you're OK*

At any time an individual will be inhabiting one of these quadrants, and it is instructive to consider how this might affect their dealings with others.

◆ *Quadrant 1 – I'm OK, you're not OK.* A person operating from this quadrant (or having this approach to life) might be seen at different times as arrogant, domineering, prejudiced, devaluing, opinionated, patronizing, rigid, impersonal, unable to listen, bureaucratic, judgemental, critical, treating others as nuisances, irritants or stupid. People in this quadrant (or life position) are often impatient, frequently negative and can be aggressive.

◆ *Quadrant 2 – You're not OK, I'm not OK.* Somebody coming from this position could be seen as low in energy, very negative, unlikely to care or take much trouble, apathetic, contributing very little, lacking commitment, unresponsive, lacking initiative and quick to accept defeat.

◆ *Quadrant 3 – You're OK, I'm not OK.* Somebody whose standpoint is from this quadrant might lack confidence, feel inadequate, play helpless, be submissive, lack sharpness and be servile and non-assertive.

◆ *Quadrant 4 – I'm OK, you're OK.* People with this standpoint are most likely to be seen as confident in themselves and others, responsive, action oriented, calm under pressure, rational, energized, creative, flexible, prepared to see others' points of view, a good listener, interested in others and working to solve problems.

Quadrant 4 is the source of all quality service.

Sometimes after an interaction or exchange between people, one person will emerge feeling superior or having gained some advantage ('winning'), while the other feels that they have somehow lost out ('losing'). In this context, winning can mean feeling that you have got the better of somebody or gained some advantage over another person. Losing can mean that you come away feeling that you have been put down, taken advantage of, or that you have been 'ridden over' in some way. In the first three quadrants, somebody loses, be it the service provider, the customer or both. In quadrant 4, both parties emerge feeling good about their interaction.

For this reason, the quadrants are sometimes given other labels:

◆ Quadrant 1 = win/lose
◆ Quadrant 2 = lose/lose
◆ Quadrant 3 = lose/win
◆ Quadrant 4 = win/win.

In quadrant 4, the service provider acts positively and confidently, using skills and talents for the benefit of the customer, because the customer is recognized as valuable and worthy of quality attention. In other quadrants there could be patterns of demeaning the customer, or of servility, which are very different from quality service.

The idea is not that anybody permanently inhabits any particular quadrant. Depending on your mood, situation and many other factors, you can occupy different quadrants at different times. The value of this concept is as follows.

◆ We have a choice of quadrants. By being aware, telling ourselves the right things and developing our skills, we can finish in quadrant 4 more often.
◆ We can invite other people to join us in quadrant 4. Our customers, as well as ourselves, will come from a variety of quadrants. By maintaining quadrant 4 behaviour, listening, being confident, responsive, clear and assertive, we can model a way of working that others will follow. We can change other people's patterns by being a shining example of how we would like them to be!

Communicating clear messages
Service providers need to pay particular attention to the skills involved in communicating clear messages. We should be aware that people cannot read our minds, so they cannot tell what we are thinking, but:

◆ they pick up messages from our behaviour – the things we do or fail to do, the things we say or do not say
◆ we are always communicating, whether we realize it or not
◆ up to 90 per cent of what we communicate will not be in words – non-verbal communication, or body language, is

often more powerful than words
◆ we may not always communicate what we intend – the skill is to get our behaviour in line with our intentions. The task at moments of truth, therefore, is to behave towards our customers in all those ways that convey the message, 'You are special'.

To give good service we need to be effective at both sending and receiving clear messages. The skills involved in sending clear messages include:

◆ knowing what we want to say
◆ deciding when and where are the appropriate time and place to say it
◆ judging how best to say it – assertively, questioningly?
◆ keeping it simple
◆ speaking clearly
◆ making eye contact
◆ monitoring the customer's response for signs of confusion, irritability, acceptance and so on
◆ using appropriate language that matches the customer's knowledge and needs
◆ making sure that what we say is consistent with how we say it (for example, not saying we're sorry through gritted teeth).

The skills involved in receiving messages from our customers include:

◆ getting rid of 'baggage', thoughts and feelings that creep in from previous events – with the last customer, with the same customer on another occasion, with a colleague, boss or concerning a home problem. Baggage will stop us giving our full, positive attention to this customer, here and now
◆ active listening, focusing entirely on what the customer is really saying
◆ checking if you're not sure what was being said
◆ listening for the feelings behind the customer's words
◆ getting rid of prejudices and assumptions about particular customers

◆ remembering that hearing something with which we disagree will mean that it is all too easy to switch off or get frustrated. When we become judgemental or begin to dislike the
customer, we are likely to have stopped listening.

 How would you describe the level of people skills and communication skills of the people in your business who are in
contact with the customer?

Showing high energy

Can you remember occasions when you have entered a shop and
the assistants have been leaning on the counter, chatting to
each other, or visited an office where someone was staring into
space looking bored or reading a newspaper. What impressions
did these occasions leave you with? Research into the skills of
making relationships shows clearly that people are attracted to
others who demonstrate high energy, look as if they are glad to
be alive, behave as if they have something to offer, and move
and work as if they have a purpose.

Of course, some people have more energy than others, and
this could have implications for who is given face-to-face contact with your customers. When picking your front-liners, pick
people who have good people skills and high energy. As Tom
Peters advises:

*Hire nice people! You can train them in other skills, but you can't
train 'nice'!*

Whatever our potential for energy, it will be affected by attitude
and lifestyle.

◆ People whose attitude to themselves and others places them
in quadrant 4 ('I'm OK, you're OK'), and possibly those

inhabiting quadrant 1, are likely to have more energy than those in the other quadrants.

◆ People who are fitter are consequently closer to their optimum energy levels, and lifestyle is important in helping to determine fitness. In general, fitter people tend to take regular exercise, do not smoke, maintain correct body weight, get seven to eight hours' sleep each night, drink alcohol moderately and eat regular meals.

This discussion of energy and fitness relates to the next and final people skill.

Working well under pressure

The satisfaction of good service flows backwards and forwards between the giver and the receiver. Achieving standards is the first challenge, maintaining them is the next. That requires particular care at times of great pressure. We can expect high service standards when people are at their best, but what about when they are not? Service providers need to be trained to develop the skills they require to look after themselves, so that they are at their best most of the time.

If you consider the word 'pressure', you are likely to have a somewhat negative reaction, linking it with words like stress, worry and anxiety. It is said that we are not at our best under pressure and that service suffers. However, service jobs need to be challenging and stimulating for us to give of our best. Tasks that are too easy, and make no demands on us, do not bring out our best performance. People who are understressed are likely to experience a lack of interest or enthusiasm for their work, and feel that what they are doing is futile. They will be bored and lacking in energy, finding it difficult to apply energy to providing service.

Conversely, tasks that are too demanding or too numerous push us into the area of too much stress. Service performance is impaired and our health can be damaged. People who are overstressed are likely to feel anxious or confused, and to experience an inability to think clearly or solve problems effectively. They will forget things and panic more easily. Their coordination will be impaired and their work will be poorly organized. Service will suffer because the provider lacks confidence and responds badly.

At our optimum level, which is neither over- nor under-stressed, we will be alert and self-confident, interested and involved in what we have to do, thinking and responding quickly. People at their optimum stress level will carry out tasks in an energetic, easy manner. They will feel good, perform well and be enthusiastic. Service excellence comes from people who are operating at this level.

There are many strategies for dealing with being either under pressure or below par.

At work:

◆ Learn good time management – organize your time so that you can accomplish your priority tasks, encouraging the important feeling of being in control.
◆ Develop problem-solving and decision-making skills – the ability to see creative solutions to difficulties and take the steps to accomplish them.
◆ Develop a support network of people to talk to – service providers can help each other by offering support and encouragement, especially at particularly pressurized times.

In general:

◆ Develop a fitness programme – there are many effective and not too time-consuming programmes that can produce a feeling of well-being. Being on top of the world is conducive to good service.
◆ Eat wholesomely – 'we are what we eat'; junk food or a generally stodgy diet does not promote the sharpness that service situations require.
◆ Learn relaxation or meditation – the ability to take the tension out of our minds and bodies can help us at difficult times.
◆ Learn constructive 'self-talk' – the ability to tell yourself positive, rational messages as a way of life, avoiding the low energy and bad feelings that result from negative 'self-talk'.

In addition, you can adopt some of the following simple but valuable tips:

◆ Work no more than 10 hours a day and five and a half days a week.
◆ Don't always strive to win.
◆ Ask for help when you need it.
◆ Set realistic deadlines that build in success.
◆ Finish one thing before starting another.
◆ Don't talk 'shop' when you are supposed to be having a break or relaxing.
◆ Learn to say 'no'; it makes your 'yes' even more valuable.
◆ Take at least 10 minutes a day to walk in the park.
◆ Allow at least 30 minutes for each meal and eat slowly.
◆ Have mini-breaks and at least one complete away-from-it-all holiday each year.
◆ Build in time for yourself, to be alone.
◆ Listen to relaxing music.
◆ Cultivate a garden.
◆ Keep a pet.
◆ Concentrate on moving, walking and talking more slowly.
◆ Avoid too many changes at once.
◆ Define any problem clearly and act early to sort it!
◆ Accept that you are not the answer to everything.
◆ Don't bottle up feelings, but avoid hostility.
◆ Have a laugh or a giggle regularly.
◆ Give yourself a treat when you have earned it, and sometimes when you have not!
◆ Be clear what your values and priorities are.

Service businesses can do a great deal to help staff manage pressure. They should, for example:

◆ offer regular skills training, on the theme of continuous service improvement – this will mean that customers are less likely to find themselves in situations that cause them to become difficult or hostile
◆ ensure that managers give good service to their staff

◆ make sure that the physical environment is comfortable and attractive to work in – this gives a clear message to staff that they are considered valuable
◆ make sure that the product or service is worth selling, so that staff can take pride in what they make or sell.

The second P – product

Good service is not a substitute for junk! If you visit a restaurant where the service is excellent, the customer is genuinely put first, the decor is very attractive, but the food is at best mediocre, it is unlikely that you will return.

Imagine that you are buying a car. The car is beautiful to look at and well presented, the staff at the dealership are attentive and helpful, the after-sales service package is superb, but the vehicle suffers from a host of faults and breaks down regularly. Three out of four aspects of your service experience were good, but you will probably still be reluctant to purchase another car from that dealer, because you now perceive its products to be of poor quality.

There is sometimes a danger that a business can become so preoccupied with developing excellent people skills that it forgets to look closely at its basic products. A customer-driven business must commit itself to continuously improving the quality of its products. In Japanese manufacturing companies, this is axiomatic. Their word for it is *kaizen*, which means 'on-going improvement involving everyone'. This means finding out what the customer wants, and then producing the goods that meet, exceed and stay ahead of those expectations.

The third P – presentation

People do judge books by their covers, and quality service businesses have to be alert to this. Customers are influenced, for better or worse, by the features that 'surround' the product or service they receive. These features can include:

◆ the physical environment that the customer enters – how does it look, sound, smell and feel, and what messages does it carry about the company's attitude to the customer?

◆ the appearance of the staff whom the customer meets
◆ the quality of brochures and marketing materials
◆ the tone and layout of correspondence
◆ the condition and appearance of company transport.

All of these will play a part in creating the customer's experience. Quality service means attending to every detail! How positive is the impact you make on your customers by:

◆ having an attractive entrance or foyer to create a stunning first impression?
◆ increasing the amount of space given over to customers by moving 'back-office' functions out of their sight?
◆ having a clear, identifiable 'house style' – reflected in logos, uniforms, colour schemes, stationery and marketing materials?
◆ introducing an attractive uniform for all customer-contact staff?

If staff feel good about their products and the place in which they work, the foundations are there for the rest of the service package.

Next time you walk into your own business premises, do so as if you were a customer entering for the first time, and describe what you see, asking yourself:

◆ What are the messages in that physical setting?
◆ Is there anything that you would want to do to change them?
◆ What about your own workspace? Does it communicate what you intend?

The fourth P – processes

In addition to continuous improvement in people skills, products and presentation, quality service means making all business processes customer driven, organizing the business so that customers can get what they want, when they want it. How often are people with excellent service skills, offering good, well-presented products, impeded by processes, practices and procedures that are less than excellent? Consider these words spoken by one service provider:

We seem to have a service black hole at head office. Our administration and technology back-up is so poor that quality service at the sharp end is undermined.

It is possible to be so focused on people skills in service provision that the way the service is organized can be overlooked.

British Telecom made customer-driven practices a priority with a massive investment in information technology. CSS (Customer Service Systems) was the world's first computer system designed to draw together all the main elements of customer service. Customers dial one number, 150, to get straight through to a single person who has everything on screen that he or she needs to take a sales order, answer an account query, report a fault or respond to any other general enquiry. The system, or process, is designed from the customer's point of view to make it easier and quicker to get what that customer wants, when he or she wants it.

So what is quality service?

A great deal of service quality is people based. People's treatment of the client, and of each other at the same time, is a key element, but it is not the whole story. The service microscope has to be focused on every dimension of the business. The way a product or service is delivered, or supplied, has to be customer driven.

◆ It is not good enough to give the customer close attention if the telephone system you use has poor reception and means a long time on hold.
◆ It is frustrating for customer-contact staff to get everything right with the customer face to face, only to find that they can't get the data they need quickly because they don't have appropriate technological back-up.
◆ It takes the edge off quality contact with the customer when paperwork goes out looking less than stylish because the office copying system is primitive.

Creating the right internal service climate will contribute to improving processes. It might also require cross-functional teams to study where blocks and hindrances to service quality are caused in business procedures. Systems and processes designed to suit the customer, rather than internal departments or functions, are the ambition.

How good are the 4 Ps in your business?

Immediate impressions, lasting impressions, impressions of all kinds are made up of many different elements – the surroundings, the service, the products and the efficiency – and we have seen how these can be categorized as the '4 Ps' of people skills, products, presentation and processes. Can you and your team make a difference in your business? The checklist in Table 4.2 encourages you to think about the 4 Ps and what you can do to improve your customers' impressions of your business.

Look at the checklist and decide where you can make a difference for each of the 4 Ps. Note what you believe you can do in each case, and add any other aspects of which you are aware. Remember that any improvement, however small, is significant and will make a difference.

In addition, you might wish to consider some of the following areas for seeking improvements:

◆ Based on their experience, could staff recommend new lines, products or services to meet customer requirements?
◆ Could displays be more imaginative, perhaps inspired by seasons, holidays or events?
◆ Can your front-line staff think what needs to be done to create a better experience for customers? What, if anything, is impeding them in offering excellent service?
◆ If uniforms are not worn, does everyone look smart and professional?
◆ How positive and impressive are the greetings and welcomes that your customers receive?
◆ Are customers served promptly? If not, what can be changed to ensure that they are?
◆ Are you able to deal with customer queries quickly and easily?

Table 4.2 *4 Ps checklist*

	Can make a difference	What I/ team can do
People skills		
Approach to greeting customers	☐	
Approach to serving customers	☐	
Approach to saying goodbye to customers	☐	
Others		
Products		
The range of products we offer	☐	
The quality of products we offer	☐	
Others		
Presentation		
Display and layout of premises	☐	
Staff appearance	☐	
My personal appearance	☐	
Others		
Processes		
The approach to serving customers	☐	
Number of staff available	☐	
Is it easy to get staff attention?	☐	
Others		

If not, is there a practice or process that is slowing down the response? Who can review this process?

Keeping customers satisfied and loyal

In Chapter 1, we established that dissatisfied customers cost businesses dearly, that today's discerning customers will move their business to a competitor if they are unhappy, and that it costs significantly more to recruit a new customer than it does to retain an existing one. So, clearly, the imperative is to keep customers not only satisfied, but loyal to your business. The effect on the 'bottom line' is when customer satisfaction results in customer retention and loyalty, which in turn generates increased profitability.

Products and services that meet requirements will satisfy customers when they are backed up by efficient service delivery. Customers will keep coming back if service delivery offers 'a little more than expected', and there is a willingness to listen to 'non-standard' requests or complaints and tackle complaints with discretion.

In summary, the challenge for every business is therefore to create customer delight and loyalty by:

◆ designing products and services that meet customer expectations – consistently
◆ delivering those products and services in a way that gives customers 'a little extra' – from personal contact and presentation to working practices (the '4 Ps')
◆ establishing mechanisms that encourage customers to comment and complain
◆ establishing a framework that allows a constructive response to 'non-standard' requests.

To fulfil these requirements, a business needs to:

◆ be clear about the business it wants to be in and which customers it wants to impress
◆ understand what customers require of its products and services

- understand their expectations of its service delivery
- measure customer satisfaction with its products and services
- identify the critical success factors that determine customer loyalty
- establish regular customer feedback mechanisms
- gather data on the value of customers and any relevant patterns
- clarify what is expected of employees and train them in what, why and how
- review its performance
- design excellent performance into management systems
- improve at least in line with customer requirements and competitor performance
- benchmark its own and its competitors' service performance.

We shall be looking at how businesses can respond to, and profit from, the opportunities created by customer complaints in a later chapter.

Team/business questionnaire 5 – moments of truth

As we have seen in this chapter, excellent service organizations understand that every contact with a customer is a moment of truth that shapes the customer's impression of the business, and strive to exceed customers' expectations at each of these moments. You now have the opportunity to score your own team or business on its moments of truth. The exercise is most valuable if all team members can complete the questionnaire individually, compare notes as a team, and then plan collective action for service improvement.

Each statement should be scored in the following way:

Score 1: if you strongly disagree that the statement is true of your business.

Score 2: if you disagree that the statement is true of your business.

Table 4.3 *Moments of truth questionnaire*

	Score
Everybody in the business is conscious of the importance of every moment of truth with customers	
We have a clear picture of what the moments of truth are with customers	
We are very clear about which staff create the customers' impression of the business	
These staff are clear that at every moment of truth there are three possible outcomes: the customer is impressed and pleased, the customer is left feeling neutral, or the customer is unimpressed and disappointed	
Front-line staff are respected; they are highly trained and well rewarded	
Front-liners feel that they are well supported by management, and colleagues in different departments and functions, in the task of providing excellent service to customers	
The business listens to front-liners, learns from them and responds to what they say	
Staff are conscious that moments of truth happen daily with internal customers and require the same skill and attention as with external customers	
Managers and team leaders are conscious of their moments of truth with their staff	
We have a clear picture of how well we perform at external and internal moments of truth	
The total possible score for moments of truth is 50	
My score for moments of truth is	

Score 3: if you see the statement as being somewhat true of your
   business.
Score 4: if you agree that the statement is true of your business.
Score 5: if you strongly agree that the statement is true of your
   business.

Three things that we could do to improve this score are:

_____

_____

Of these, the most important is:

_____

_____

Team/business questionnaire 6 – the 4 Ps

A business that is committed to excellent service knows that its
customers' experience is shaped by people, products, presentation and processes. All these aspects of service are monitored
and continually improved to ensure that the customer's overall
experience is one of delight. You now have the opportunity to
score your own team or business on its 4 Ps. The exercise is most
valuable if all team members can complete the questionnaire.

Three things that we could do to improve this score are:

_____

_____

Of these, the most important is:

_____

_____

Table 4.4 *4 Ps questionnaire*

	Score
People are very conscious that the customer's experience is made positive or negative by four factors: people skills, quality of products and services, features of our presentation, and our processes to deliver what customers want	
The people skills of our front-liners, their ability to make customers feel special, are of a very high order	
The quality of products and services is excellent and invariably meets customers' requirements	
Features of the presentation of the business to customers – premises, paperwork, brochures, advertising and staff appearance – are very good	
Processes, practices and procedures are designed from the customer's point of view and are extremely customer friendly	
We are continuously improving the quality of products and services	
We are continuously improving how we present the business to customers	
We are continuously improving processes, practices and procedures so that they are customer friendly and cost effective	
Standards exist throughout the business defining required levels of performance in each of the 4 Ps	
The total possible score for the 4 Ps is 50	
My score for the 4 Ps is	

5

Setting and Measuring Service Standards

Recent research into how we use our brains has highlighted the fact that each of us works predominantly in either the right or the left brain hemisphere. The characteristics of right- or left-brain thinkers, it is suggested, are as shown in Table 5.1.

Table 5.1 *Brain hemispheres*

Left brain	Right brain
Logical	Free flowing
Sequential	Whole picture
Data based	Feelings before facts
Looks at detail	Creative
Verbal	Spontaneous
Deductive	People centred
Rational	Pictures before words

One hemisphere is not superior to the other; they each offer different gifts. The problem in a service context comes when we work out of one hemisphere and close our minds to people who see things differently. Right-brain thinkers will be attracted by the creativity, energy and passion of quality service, for example; left-brain thinkers will need the detail, the facts and the proof that it is working. Both are important.

You could ask the designer of a quality service programme:

◆ How will you recognize that your programme is working?
◆ How will you prove to the finance director (likely to be an extremely competent left-brain thinker) that your investment is worthwhile?

◆ Will you expect quality improvements in every part of the business or only where people are enthused and volunteer?
◆ What does excellence or quality look like or consist of?

Those may seem like mischievous questions, but they do require a shift from right to left brain, and quality service calls for a whole-brain approach. We have to move from passion and enthusiasm to detail, clarity and specifics! In all businesses there will be left- and right-brain thinkers, who need to be persuaded and motivated in their own terms. This means that we need to be able to talk about standards to create a common ground between creativity and practical delivery.

This chapter therefore focuses on standard setting and measuring in a service business, by leading you through the following key concepts:

◆ the meaning of service standards and why they are useful
◆ setting service standards
◆ measuring performance against the 4 Ps
◆ using the P–D–C–A cycle in setting and measuring standards.

Two further questionnaires appear at the end of the chapter, in order for you to rate your team or business on its:

◆ quality service standards
◆ measurement.

What is a service standard?

Chambers 20th Century Dictionary defines a standard as:

A basis of measurement, a criterion, an established or accepted model, a definite level of excellence or adequacy required, aimed at, or possible.

The key words in the definition are:

- ◆ *measurement* – the standards must be measurable
- ◆ *accepted model* – the standards are agreed by everyone
- ◆ *definite level* – the standards do not change from person to person, or level to level. They are fair and consistent.

If we visualize an advanced quality service business, it is sure to have the following features:

- ◆ a commitment to quality performance by everybody, at every level, in every area
- ◆ an understanding by everybody of what represents quality service in the eyes of their customers, internal as well as external
- ◆ a translation of those expectations into specific performance standards that are the basis of assessment and reward.

Service standards help ensure that a team or business is fit to compete at the highest level. An athlete needs to improve her performance if she is going to win the next race. She sets herself a series of targets, over a period of time, which will build up her ability. She also sets several smaller, more detailed and specific targets to help her achieve each of the main targets, such as stamina and endurance. She then measures and monitors her progress and continually checks her technique for achieving the targets. This may require a tiny improvement or a major rethink of her methods. When she has taken part in the race, she will begin again to plan her strategy for the next competition. If she has lost the race, she may completely rethink her training schedule. Even if she has won, she will still have to work hard to maintain, and even exceed, that performance.

Organizations can set themselves performance-improvement targets and standards, just as an athlete can. Similarly, there is always another goal to aim at – even if it is the tiniest improvement, like the athlete's extra 100th of a second off her previous personal best.

Why have service standards?

Service standards are one of the most crucial components of the quality service process. Without them, any service initiative may not be able to maintain itself.

What do you think might be the benefits of setting and working to service standards?

For the customer?

_____

_____

For you?

_____

_____

For the business as a whole?

_____

_____

Where service standards exist, customers know what to expect. They can be confident that the product or service will meet their needs and that it will be reliable. They will find doing business with the organization pleasant and easy, and high standards will help attract and retain discerning customers.

Individual service providers also know where they stand in terms of what is expected from them and what they are aiming for. The achievement of high standards increases job satisfaction. The performance of staff is measured fairly, because it is based on specific criteria, rather than a personal interpretation of performance.

The organization as a whole will find that standards help achieve the best results, they are something to aim for and encourage continuous improvement. Standards help maintain good working practices and performance can be measured against the standards. Above all, standards save time and money, as they help reduce:

◆ wasted energy and effort pursuing peripheral activity
◆ poorly produced or scrapped goods
◆ the amount of rework needed
◆ follow-up services required
◆ customer frustration or dissatisfaction.

Service standards matter because they enable us to make concrete those factors that comprise quality. This clarity makes achievement more likely and measurement possible. Standards also provide a foundation that can be upgraded at intervals, as we develop and improve service to meet ever-increasing customer discernment.

The cost of doing it wrong

It is difficult to calculate the exact cost of doing things wrong, mainly because there are so many complex ways in which both time and money can be lost. However, research has shown that up to 30 per cent of a business's income can be lost because of a failure to set and achieve quality standards. How many of the following time and money losers can you identify in your own business?

◆ Are faulty goods and services rejected by customers asking for refunds or replacements?
◆ Are there significant numbers of people dealing with customer complaints or servicing issues?
◆ Does work have to be redone because mistakes are made?
◆ Are products scrapped because they are not produced properly?
◆ Do components have to be returned to suppliers because they are not delivered as specified?

◆ Do new work processes fail to operate as expected and have to be redesigned or reprogrammed?

If you have answered 'yes' to any of these, it means that your organization's service standards could be improved, or new standards introduced, to avoid these situations in future.

How service standards can help

A business committed to a service quality programme will soon see a reduction in the amount of time and money spent on correcting service failures. After an initial period of higher cost and time investment in service improvement, it will similarly find that the cost of recovering from less than impressive service reduces. Quality service companies do invest in training employees and in setting up specialist quality service systems, with the aim that initial investment will eventually reduce the costs of failure, corrective action and checking.

Cost savings through setting and achieving service standards will benefit everyone:

◆ *The customer* – the price of goods or services can be maintained or even reduced, while service quality is improved.
◆ *The company* – there is less wasted effort and rework, and there are more customers!
◆ *The individual* – employed by an organization that is working towards a more secure and prosperous future.

How to set standards

Wherever possible, the following principles should underpin the development of quality service standards:

◆ They should be decided after dialogue with customers, learning what they want, expect and regard as impressive, and after studying the competition.
◆ They should be decided in dialogue with those who have to work to the standards, not simply handed down from on high.

◆ They should start with those areas of the business that have the most impact on the external customer, but should eventually address service between internal customers and suppliers.

◆ They should address 'soft' as well as 'hard' aspects of service. 'Soft' standards are the people, or expressive, side of quality, such as the warmth of greetings and the courtesy and politeness of staff. Research evidence across a range of businesses confirms the importance of soft standards as a differentiator for customers. It seems that 'hard' standards, such as the time taken to provide a service or deliver a product, have the capacity to dissatisfy a customer if we fail to meet expectations, but are unlikely to impress or excite if we get them right. Far more powerful to customers are the soft standards that amount to quality attention, make them feel special and that they are treated as individuals.

To understand how quality service standards work in practice, consider the following scenarios:

◆ *Scenario A* – The personnel manager of a large financial organization gives receptionists the following instructions: 'We want to be the most welcoming company there is, so do everything you can to create an excellent impression for the customers.'

◆ *Scenario B* – The personnel manager outlines the same aims to the reception team. She then sits down with the team to identify the goals they want to reach, to define exactly what comprises an excellent impression, before forming a specific plan of how they can reach their chosen service standards.

 Which of the two approaches do you believe is most likely to result in long-term improvement in the quality of service given to customers by the reception staff?

Approach B is, of course, much more likely to produce the best result. The staff are asked for their input and clear standards emerge from their involvement. Setting standards in this way puts people in a much better position to deliver them because:

◆ the standards are clear and identifiable
◆ the team has worked together to form the standards
◆ people have a plan to follow so they know how and when they aim to reach the standards
◆ managers and team leaders find their jobs easier when standards are clearly defined.

What sort of service standards might the team of receptionists and their manager have set for themselves? Consider your own business and the quality of customer service you would like to see offered to your customers by reception staff.

You will probably have included some of the following:

◆ We will keep the reception area bright, clean and attractive.
◆ Fresh tea and coffee will always be available for visitors, as will a selection of reading materials.
◆ We will be polite and friendly when welcoming customers and use their names when speaking to them.
◆ We will give customers our full attention when they arrive.
◆ We will not talk among ourselves when visitors are present.
◆ We will answer calls within four rings, give the company name and our own name and note all essential information about the call.
◆ We will transfer calls only when we are clear who the customer needs to speak with, to avoid transferring the customer from department to department.

Performance in the 4 Ps

Now that you have a better understanding of what service standards are, and of some of the tools employed in setting them, it is useful to focus for a moment on your own situation. Identify the service standards that already exist in your business and, secondly, in your team in particular. These are likely to relate to the way you deal with customers, such as responding to letters within 24 hours, or answering the telephone within four rings. Additionally, they may relate to the way things look, such as keeping work areas tidy. There may be standards relating to the goods or services themselves, the way they are designed, produced or delivered.

What are your business's service standards?

_____

What are your team's service standards?

_____

_____

It is useful to categorize service standards into the four areas described by the 4 Ps – people, products, presentation and processes. Categorizing standards allows you to identify particular areas of strength and weakness and to ensure that the standards you are setting are relevant to the customer's experience of your business.

◆ *People standards.* These will relate to the way in which customers, including internal customers, are treated by the people in your organization. Quality people standards describe how people behave towards customers, building good relationships and customer loyalty.

◆ *Product standards.* These are the standards promised to customers relating to any products or services that they receive.
◆ *Presentation standards.* Service standards in this area will be concerned with such factors as the appearance of work areas, the smartness of staff, the design of company logos, the packaging of the product and anything else that is seen, or experienced, by customers.
◆ *Process standards.* These are concerned with the way in which processes and procedures are designed and organized in the business, and will cover areas such as how customers buy goods and receive bills.

Look at the standards that exist in your business, and those that you have identified for improvement, and categorize each of them into one of the 4 Ps (Table 5.2).

Table 5.2 *Standards and the 4 Ps*

Which P?	Service standard
People	
Products	
Presentation	
Processes	

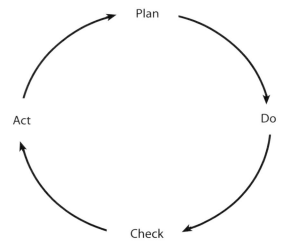

Figure 5.1 *P–D–C–A cycle*

The P-D-C-A cycle

Quality guru Dr W. Edwards Deming designed a process for the implementation of service quality standards. Each stage is necessary for overall success. It can be used to create a masterplan for a whole organization, and also to create departmental or team service standards. This process is known as the P–D–C–A cycle (Figure 5.1):

◆ *Plan* – decide what you want to achieve and gather the information you need to help you achieve it.
◆ *Do* – implement the plan.
◆ *Check* – check that your plan has achieved the intended result.
◆ *Act* – act on the results of your checking process and begin the cycle again.

P-D-C-A cycle stage 1 – plan

You will need to gather a great deal of information when you begin to form service standard improvement plans. For instance, you will need to identify any existing standards and find out the current level of customer satisfaction. You will need information on some or all of the following:

◆ what customers and staff think about your product or service and the improvements that they would like to see
◆ who your competitors are, their strengths, weaknesses and offerings to their customers
◆ whether staff are trained to meet the existing and proposed standards
◆ whether your budget is adequate
◆ whether the correct, necessary equipment is available.

Gathering this information will reveal where you can start to form your service standard improvement plans. Only when you have done all the research can you set objectives and draw up action plans.

Customer opinions – internal and external

You will need data to enable you to identify the kind of service standards that your customers, internal and external, expect from your team or your business. Once you have a clear picture of these requirements, you can begin to plan and implement service standard improvements. Setting new service standards may require the help of other departments, so first ask the following questions:

◆ Who do we rely on to provide us with service, to enable us in turn to be able to deliver improved service standards?
◆ Do we need to agree new service standards with other teams or organizations?

You may then need to contact and discuss your requirements with the necessary internal and external suppliers.

Before setting service standard goals, you also need to gather information about how customers judge your current standards. As we have emphasized already, it is important to find out directly what they feel about your products or services. You can gather information by asking a cross-section, or representative number, of your customers:

◆ how they rate the standards of your products and services
◆ what they would like to see done better

◆ in which areas they particularly wish to see improvements
◆ their advice or ideas about what else you should be striving for in pursuit of even higher service standards.

You may also find it useful to analyse the number and type of the complaints that your business or team receives that are generated by poor standards.

Front-line staff work very closely with customers and are likely to have a fairly accurate perception of your customers' views about the business, so it is worth canvassing their opinions about the improvements that they believe customers would wish to see. Customer-facing staff should also be surveyed to ascertain the service standards they are delivering now, the standards they want to deliver in the future, and the training and support they will need to enable them to reach these standards.

In stressing the importance of involving people in setting the standards to which you need them to work, the intention is not to preclude essential management input into standards, merely to advise that standards should not be set wholly by either management or staff, but should rather emerge from the troika of customers, management and staff.

As a team, you can gather all the information and suggested standards and start the process of deciding which service standard objectives to set, being particularly guided by information on the following:

◆ problems that have cropped up again and again
◆ actions which have lost customers
◆ problems caused by technical error and those caused by human error.

Once you have reviewed the information that you have gathered, record at least three ideas for service improvements that have emerged.

The key thing to remember about setting standards is that they need to be clear and precise. For instance, 'We will reduce customer complaints by 10 per cent during the next two months' is clearer and more specific than, 'We will improve our service quality'.

You have identified areas for which you are considering setting standards in your own business. For each standard, it is necessary to go through the following checklist:

1 State the proposed standard clearly and specifically, starting with the word 'to' followed by an action word. For instance, 'To ensure that all written customer queries are answered within 48 hours'.

Our standard will be 'To…:

_____

_____

2 State the date by which you want your new standard to be in place.

We will operate to our new standard from:

_____

_____

3 Make sure that other people will find the standard acceptable.

We have checked that the following people/groups are committed to this standard:

_____

_____

4   Identify any constraints that may make the standard difficult to achieve. If there are constraints, you may need to
monitor these factors regularly.

Constraints that we will monitor are:

———

5   Identify any resources that will be particularly significant in
helping you achieve the standard.

The following resources will help us achieve our standard:

———

Prioritizing standard setting

Every organization is different and each will have many different standards to set. Most companies simply don't have the
resources to tackle all their service problems at once, so before
they begin setting service standards they need to be clear which
will make the biggest impact, while at the same time remaining
achievable, by considering the following:

◆   *The bigger picture* – which standards will do most to help us
    achieve our business priorities?
◆   *Timing* – going for early success creates enthusiasm and spurs
    people on to greater things.
◆   *Impact* – which service standards will have the most impact
    in terms of customer service, cost savings and staff morale?
◆   *Interdepartmental support* – new standards that require input
    from more than one department can be complicated, but they

may have a wide effect across the business. They also demonstrate the importance of working together for service success.

◆ *The seriousness of the problem* – are poor standards in one area causing the most severe difficulties? If so, this area may need to be tackled first.

P-D-C-A cycle stage 2 – do

Once you have outlined and prioritized your plans for service standards, achieving them may seem straightforward. However, there are additional factors that you need to look out for once your plans go into action. Keep ensuring that you:

◆ understand your customers' requirements
◆ make sure that your suppliers, internal and external, are clear about your requirements
◆ gather data that will enable you to judge the success of your performance
◆ work with colleagues to solve any problems that arise.

P-D-C-A cycle stage 3 – check

The importance of measurement

Good service standards have built-in checking devices. These include regular gathering of statistical information, which can be analysed to judge whether standards are being reached and maintained. Bear in mind that too much data can be confusing. Usually, the only data needed is that measuring success and reliability and predicting future performance. This information is then fed back to staff at reviews. Regular meetings provide opportunities to review performance against that of other departments, as well as in terms of the organization's overall aims.

What other benefits would you foresee for your own business in regular measurement and review?

Your suggestions might have included the following:

◆ Problems can be spotted quickly and corrected.
◆ Meetings encourage teamwork and better communication.
◆ Regular feedback lets people know how they are performing.
◆ Requests for more time, people and resources can be considered.

What to measure

It is vital to be able to measure the extent of your achievement against your service standards. For each standard, you need to be able to identify how you are going to carry out checks or measure progress. There are many ways to measure changes resulting from the successful setting of service standards, and you need to decide these methods of measurement for each standard. They will include:

◆ customer satisfaction forms for internal and external customers
◆ analyses of sales and profit increases
◆ calculating the decrease in the amount of recovery undertaken, or in time spent correcting mistakes (it will be necessary to develop a system for recording the time spent on these tasks)
◆ quantifying changes in staff attitude – for example, it is possible to measure reductions in absenteeism or lateness
◆ recording reductions in the number of returned goods or complaints.

The value of measurement is that once progress has been achieved, further development can be undertaken in pursuit of continuous improvement.

P-D-C-A cycle stage 4 – act

Using measurement to drive performance

Quality measurement will nearly always lead to further action. Standards need to be seen as the foundation on which you build.

They must not be set in concrete and treated as immutable. Even the most minor adjustment is a valuable part of the service standard improvement process. When a change has been proven, it becomes the new standard, which in turn can be improved. Your business, your people and your customers are continuously acquiring greater awareness and sophistication. Quality service is about continuous improvement and your standards will grow as you do, becoming higher and more demanding.

So once progress has been checked and the need for further improvements identified, more plans have to be made, and so the P–D–C–A cycle begins again!

The journey to excellence is a journey … not a destination!

Learning from experience: two case studies

Case study 1 – an airline
The problem: It was recognized that standards were vital because major competitors were working successfully to them, but low staff morale meant that there would be resistance to anything from 'on high'.

The decision: Take evidence of customer research plus competition standards to selected groups of staff who provided service in-flight and on the ground, and ask them to write standards for their own performance.

The result: Ownership of the standards document, with a clear recognition that it must be the customer who sets the standards!

Case study 2 – a building society
The problem: Staff believed that customers wanted a reply within three days when applying for a home loan. They put tremendous pressure on themselves and the business to deliver this as standard.

The reality: The marketing department carried out customer research showing that only a small percentage of customers actually appreciated such a turnaround. A high proportion felt that they would have been happy with a standard of seven to ten days, because this would give them time to re-evaluate their decision to buy, and they felt that it was more likely to have been done properly, with no short-cuts.

The lesson: Guessing what will impress customers can mean providing more than they want. Sometimes, of course, customers do have unrealistic expectations and it may be necessary to 'educate' them to appreciate the value in the service standards offered. Thoroughness and a guarantee of accuracy may be more attractive to most customers than speed of turnaround.

Team/business questionnaire 7 – quality service standards

Excellent service businesses realize the crucial role that the setting and review of service standards can play in driving quality service performance. They understand the benefits brought about for the business, its customers and the individuals involved in service delivery, and the pay-off in terms of customer loyalty. Quality service standards also reduce the cost of correcting errors and handling complaints.

You now have the opportunity to score your own team or business on its quality service standards (Table 5.3). The exercise is of most value if all team members can complete the questionnaire and then compare their perspectives and plan improvements.

Each statement should be scored in the following way:

Score 1: if you strongly disagree that the statement is true of your business.
Score 2: if you disagree that the statement is true of your business.
Score 3: if you see the statement as being somewhat true of your business.

Table 5.3 *Quality service standards questionnaire*

	Score
Quality service standards exist in every part of the business	☐
The standards address soft as well as hard service standards	☐
Service standards are worked out in dialogue with customers, and address what they regard as critical success factors	☐
Service standards are established in dialogue with staff and are not simply handed down from the top	☐
We regularly review performance against standards and communicate the findings to staff	☐
We know that the standards we offer customers compare with those offered by competitors	☐
We regularly review standards and seek to upgrade them	☐
Standards exist for internal service between people and departments in-house	☐
Service standards are part of the performance management system and individuals are appraised against them	☐
Performance against standards is linked to a reward system	☐
The total possible score for quality service standards is 50	
My score for quality service standards is	☐

Score 4: if you agree that the statement is true of your business.
Score 5: if you strongly agree that the statement is true of your business.

Three things that we could do to improve this score are:

_____

_____

Of these, the most important is:

_____

_____

Team/business questionnaire 8 – measurement

The setting of quality service standards is the beginning of a cycle of continuous improvement. Excellent service businesses review their performance against the standards and seek further improvement. This can only be done when it is clear how performance against standards is to be measured or quantified.

You now have the opportunity to score your own team or business on its measurement of performance (Table 5.4). The exercise is most valuable if all team members can complete the questionnaire, decide their individual view, compare notes and plan improvements together.

Three things that we could do to improve this score are:

_____

_____

Of these, the most important is:

_____

_____

Table 5.4 *Measurement questionnaire*

	Score
We regard measurement of performance as a cornerstone of service excellence	☐
We are clear what the critical success factors are in the eyes of customers and measure performance against them	☐
We measure customer satisfaction regularly and in a range of ways	☐
We use findings from measurement activities to educate staff and inform management decisions	☐
We have clear goals and regularly measure achievements against them	☐
We measure internal service performance as a basis for continuous improvement	☐
We regularly monitor staff attitudes and opinions	☐
We measure the service performance of individual departments and functions, as distinct from our overall performance	☐
We use staff opinions and internal service measures to inform management performance and decision making	☐
We are continually seeking to upgrade the quality and scope of measurement factors affecting our customers	☐

The total possible score for measurement is 50

My score for measurement is	☐

6

PROFITING FROM COMPLAINTS

No one likes to hear complaints, whether the criticism is about themselves or the business for which they work, but we need to learn to treasure them. Complaints can be the lifeblood of our business. That may sound extreme, but what does it mean if you never have complaints?

◆ Your service is perfect?
◆ Your customers are too frightened to complain – they just go away?
◆ Your customers just cannot be bothered to complain – and they go away too?
◆ Your customers have tried complaining and nothing changes – so they also leave?

One thing of which you can be sure is that however hard you and your team work, your service will never be perfect. People will always be too individual for your service package to appeal to everyone in your target group at all times. Your aim should be to reduce a torrent of complaints to a trickle, but if that trickle dries up, rather than sitting around congratulating yourselves, you should begin to ask, 'Are we missing something?'.

Complaints can be the educators of your business. Your biggest problem will be unearthing them.

This chapter examines the crucial role played by customer complaints in driving continuous service improvement, and introduces a number of key concepts in customer service:

◆ bringing complaints to light
◆ seeing complaints positively and turning them into opportunities

◆ handling complaints
◆ recovering from complaints
◆ setting up a complaints system.

The chapter concludes with a questionnaire, providing an opportunity to rate your own team or business on the extent to which it currently profits from customer complaints.

What do the facts tell us about complaints? Technical Assistance Research Programmes (TARP) of Washington DC investigated customer behaviour in over 200 companies in the US and Canada, and found the following:

◆ Most dissatisfied customers do not complain. Senior management in the average business does not hear from 96 per cent of its unhappy customers.
◆ For every complaint received, there will be another 26 customers with problems, and at least six of these will be serious.
◆ People often don't complain because they think it is not worth the time and effort, they don't know how or where to complain, or they believe that the company would be indifferent to them.
◆ People who don't complain are precisely those who are least likely to buy from the company again. A complainer who gets a response is more likely to come back. Between 65 and 90 per cent of non-complainers will never buy from you again and you won't know why.
◆ When customers complain and the matter is dealt with satisfactorily, 54 per cent will buy again. If a complaint is dealt with quickly and efficiently, the retention rate rises to 90 to 95 per cent. These figures relate to major purchases such as cars and domestic appliances.
◆ In the case of smaller purchases like food and clothing, 37 per cent of unhappy non-complainers will not purchase again, whereas 82 per cent of complainers will, if their complaint is handled well.
◆ Damage is not restricted to the person with a complaint. A customer who has had an unpleasant experience will tell an

average of nine to ten other people, and 13 per cent of those with a complaint will tell more than 20 others.

◆ When a complainer has had a satisfactory response, they will tell only half the number of other people and will talk about the experience positively.

These facts about customer behaviour make it clear that it is better to have complaints than silent dissatisfaction!

How to unearth complaints

Researching your customers in an ongoing way is one method of ensuring that you identify needs, but it also begins to unearth irritants and, best of all, potential irritants before they develop into fully fledged problems. There are many different ways to do this – some systematic, some non-systematic, some boring, some fun. It is important to get the right balance.

Systematic methods include the following:

◆ Customer surveys – random, or using a quota-sampling technique. You might send out questionnaires to customers at regular intervals after they have bought a product or service, checking their happiness or otherwise with the experience.

◆ Telephone surveys. These are increasingly popular, and might take the form of a call to a random selection of customers each month or quarter.

◆ Staff surveys. These tap into all the customer intelligence that staff possess. It is especially useful to survey front-liners to check what, if anything, customers are less than happy with in their experience.

◆ Setting up a centralized system so that all complaints are recorded, monitored, analysed and regularly reported on.

◆ Monitoring the performance of staff using 'mystery shoppers' – people who pose as customers in person or on the telephone. This is a technique that should only be used after careful consideration, and with the backing of staff.

Non-systematic methods might include the following:

◆ Video points. These are booths, a little like those you sit inside to take your own passport photograph. Once inside, the customer is invited to make a video of themselves talking to the company about how they have found the service, what was pleasing and anything that was less so.

◆ Customer hotlines. Some research suggests that these are among the most effective methods. A useful practice is to organize periodic meetings of telephone-answering staff to discuss their sense of what is happening in the marketplace.

◆ Feedback cards. Quite common in hotels, these are cards that customers can fill out quickly to record their feelings about the service. As an incentive to complete the cards, some companies will enter them into a prize draw at regular intervals.

Some of these techniques become talking points and, as such, can help build a positive image for the company, as well as potentially being the germs of new service ideas. However, non-systematic methods largely rely on the customer taking the initiative in responding to an invitation to give feedback. We know from the TARP findings just how difficult it can be to get customers to do this, and therefore the techniques often need to be a little gimmicky to attract customers to give up their time. The problem with this is that gimmicky techniques tend to attract people who like gimmicks! Having said that, some of the techniques certainly do provide customer data – the problem comes in not knowing how representative it is.

Whatever method, or combination of methods, is used, service businesses need to keep in close touch with their customers' feelings to ensure that they remain customers. So it is crucial to learn how to receive, respond and turn complaints round. It makes sense to use the opportunity constructively, to see a complaint as a second chance to get it right. Handling complaints takes sensitivity and tact when you are on the receiving end. It also takes skill and professionalism.

Seeing complaints positively

Before you are able to think positively about complaints, improve the way you respond to them and see how you can profit from them, you need to gain an understanding of how well complaints are currently handled by your team or business.

How well do you deal with complaints now?

You are invited to use the checklist in Table 6.1 to evaluate the current complaint-handling skills of your team or business, and to pinpoint areas for improvement. Place a tick against any of the statements that are true of your business.

It is very difficult to get 10 ticks on this checklist. If you have, then you must be totally professional, with few faults, and have people with a great deal of experience. However, there are still likely to be areas for improvement. Review the checklist and consider which areas these might be.

If you have 8–9 ticks – this is an almost perfect score. The people in your business must be confident, positive and able to cope well with difficult situations.

If you have 6–8 ticks – good. Although this is promising, a little more work on several areas would not go amiss.

If you have 4–6 ticks – there is a need to work to improve overall attitudes and performance to deal effectively with complaining customers. You will need to pinpoint the areas requiring attention as you work through this chapter.

If you have fewer than 4 ticks – this is a challenge! Work needs to be done on skills for dealing with complaints. This chapter will help you identify the areas that most need attention and, with practice, improvements will come about.

A low score should not discourage you. As long as there is keenness to improve, the necessary awareness and skills can soon be learned. Experience is a very important factor when dealing with complaints.

Table 6.1 *Complaints checklist*

We are:	Tick if true
Always pleasant to customers, even if they are not pleasant to us	☐
Always ready to welcome suggestions from customers and colleagues about how we could improve	☐
Able to receive and handle complaints without feeling personally attacked	☐
Able to smile when we don't feel like it	☐
Always able to apologize to a customer, even if we are not at fault	☐
Willing to listen carefully and sympathetically to customers and find out what they want	☐
Able to give reasons and positive suggestions when we cannot do exactly what the customer wants	☐
Able to keep calm and behave professionally if a customer becomes upset	☐
Able to calm a customer if necessary and involve colleagues if any of us becomes upset	☐
Able to recover and profit from complaints and ensure that the customer goes away feeling that we were helpful, we solved the problem satisfactorily and wanting to return	☐

Total no. of ticks
☐

Write down any particular areas that you have identified for improvement:

Turning complaints into opportunities

A company needs to welcome complaints as a second chance to keep a customer.

When you think of the term 'complain', you are likely to associate it with negative words or phrases. However, there is a positive way of looking at complaints. In fact, looking positively at complaints is the first step on the way to dealing positively with them.

Your attitude to your customers and their complaints has to be a positive one before you even start to deal with the problems they describe. It is necessary to be able to deal professionally and positively with the situation and see it as a second chance to give even better service.

Take a moment to think of three reasons that complaints may be valuable or to be welcomed.

Every point of contact, every moment of truth with a customer, is a chance to impress that customer, build the relationship and encourage them to return. A complaint is another moment of truth and one that can be used particularly effectively.

Research on complaints carried out by one major airline revealed that customers whose complaints were dealt with efficiently and politely felt more positive about the company than they did when everything was right in the first place. Even a complaint made but not satisfactorily dealt with makes the customer 10 per cent more likely to come back – just being able to complain helps. This is not to suggest that mistakes should be made just so they can be put right, but that a complaint is an excellent opportunity to give a customer that little more than they expect when it is put right. Recovery is very impressive. This is the positive way of looking at complaints.

Handling complaints

A customer with the passion to get angry also has the ability to be loyal.

The best starting point is to put yourself in the customer's place and analyse the feelings behind the complaint.

Think like a customer

When dealing with complaints, it is essential to bear in mind the customer's attitudes and feelings. Consider the last time you had to return a faulty item to a store, or advise a bank, garage or insurance company that it had made a mistake. Remember how you felt.

How did you feel when you discovered the fault or problem?

How did you feel when you decided to do something about it?

How did you feel as you did so? Did you have to brace yourself when you picked up the telephone or approached the sales person, for instance?

Typically, the customer's three-stage reaction is as follows:

◆ Stage 1: Irritation and frustration at not being able to use the item straight away.

◆ Stage 2: Annoyance at having to waste time taking it back or complaining – wondering whether they should or not, whether they can make time for it or whether it is worth it at all.

◆ Stage 3: A customer has to feel brave to go through with the complaint, so they might have to summon up courage to do it while they are still angry. People often feel unsure of themselves when they complain and this can make them more aggressive, as well as extra-sensitive to the response that they receive.

The result is that when we deal with complaints, we could be dealing with someone who is angry or annoyed, rude or aggressive. We might be dealing with someone who feels uncertain of themselves, who will be very easily irritated if our response is rude or offhand.

The importance of an apology
You must apologize at once, whether it is your fault or not.

You are not taking the blame when you apologize. You are simply apologizing on behalf of the company for what has happened. Responses like 'I wasn't here at the time' or 'I don't know anything about this' are a waste of time and only make the situation worse. Customers see you as a representative of the organization and so you must live up to their expectations. Even if the customer does need to speak to somebody else, it is still important to listen and sympathize, apologize immediately, and explain what you will do to solve the problem, before you find the right person to deal with it. That way, the customer is more likely to stay calm and feel able to put his or her complaint reasonably.

Keep cool, be polite and reassuring and, above all, never argue with a customer. Professionalism in these situations involves keeping your head when your customers are losing theirs and blaming it on you!

A plan for dealing with complaints

Experience suggests that the following should be included in any set of guidelines on managing complaints:

◆ Recognize the customer's feelings and listen carefully.
◆ Collect all data and details.
◆ Accept responsibility; don't pass the buck.
◆ Find out what the customer wants, work out what you can do and do it quickly.
◆ If there is something you can't do, say so and explain why.
◆ Work out how to give that little bit more.
◆ Don't, whatever the provocation, argue with your customer.
◆ Check that the customer is satisfied with any outcome and thank him or her for bringing the problem to your attention.
◆ Work out what you or your team can learn from the experience and how you can stop it happening again.
◆ If appropriate, make contact with the customer at a later date – perhaps by means of a telephone call or letter to ask about his or her current experience with your service or product.

The 10-point plan that follows can be used as a framework to assist front-line staff in handling customer complaints:

1 Apologize.
2 Listen carefully – get the facts and the details.
3 Sympathize – show that you understand the problem. Show that you have heard their complaint.
4 Don't guess at an answer if you don't know it.
5 Accept responsibility – don't pass the buck. You are not saying that it is your fault. You are apologizing and dealing with the complaint on behalf of the company.
6 Take action – pass the complaint on to someone else or deal with it yourself.
7 Tell the customer what you are doing – if the process is taking longer than you thought it would, go back and apologize for the delay. Explain what is happening.
8 Keep calm, be polite and provide assurance that you are willing to help and that the problem will not recur.

9 Don't argue – if the customer is upsetting you and making you angry, and you can't avoid being dragged into an argument, involve someone else. Quite often, bringing in another person will defuse the situation.
10 Above all, be professional, calm, focused, attentive and problem solving.

Responding effectively to complaints

At some time, people will wish to complain about your service. This is normal and you should expect it. At that moment, attitude is the key to success. It is not easy to listen to criticism, particularly if it is not made skilfully. It is easy to be dismissive or defensive and to ignore or retaliate. If we are observant enough, we will be able to detect our 'self-talk'. We all talk to ourselves in our heads and tell ourselves things that may produce problems. Self-talk can be positive or negative. We will respond and react as a result of what we tell ourselves. Appropriate self-talk when managing complaints could be:

◆ 'I wish that had not happened, but I am pleased that the customer has told me as this gives me a second chance.'
◆ 'A complaint is a moment of truth, a service opportunity. I'll try to be impressive.'
◆ 'This is not pleasant to hear, but it is a chance to learn.'

It is possible to make situations involving complaints easier and more bearable by controlling the way we respond. The sequence of responses to any situation follows a pattern:

◆ Stage 1: Something happens.
◆ Stage 2: You respond.
◆ Stage 3: There are consequences.

Although we are not always in control of Stage 1, what happens initially, we can influence Stage 3, the outcome, by the way we react at Stage 2.

On hearing a complaint we can respond in one of three ways:

◆ *The aggressive (or quadrant 1) response.* We express our feelings and opinions so forcibly that the customer feels threatened, punished or put down. Our intention, when we are behaving like this, is to get our own way no matter what the consequences. To achieve this we can be verbally violent, manipulative or devious. If we win and get what we want, the customer may be left with feelings of bitterness, resentment or frustration. Because we have caused the customer to lose, he or she may want revenge and get it by telling people about the experience. Their custom will be lost and they will take others with them as they recount the experience.

◆ *The passive (or quadrant 3) response.* Here we avoid the issue, running away or ducking problems rather than facing them and solving them. We allow ourselves to be treated without dignity or rights. We might apologize, but will not take action and will not reassure the customer. A whining tone of voice and feeble body language might back up what is being said – often something like 'There's nothing we can do' or 'It's not my fault, it's nothing to do with me'. The likely outcome of this is that we will emerge feeling bad about ourselves and the customer, whom we will blame for our discomfort. The customer comes away from this experience feeling let down and angry.

◆ *The assertive response.* We are assertive and confident, we face the issue and try to find a solution. We recognize the customer's right to complain and welcome the complaint as a positive contribution to achieving quality of service. We accept responsibility without crawling and seek a win/win solution that will satisfy the customer and please us, because it is also in our interests. Recognizing our own rights, as well as those of the customer, means that we are likely to emerge from the experience feeling that we have done our best and have satisfied the customer as far as possible. The customer feels reassured and confident that the complaint has been heard and dealt with as well as possible under the circumstances. That is often the most important part of the process.

We can work hard to ensure that, as service providers, we approach our customers from quadrant 4. There are, of course, no guarantees that this is where our customers will come from! If they are quadrant 4 people, you have a flying start; if they are not, there is work ahead!

Not everything will go consistently as we plan it. Not every customer comes with the same expectations. Given those realities, however hard you work, you will not please all of the people all of the time!

Being assertive

Being assertive does not mean standing up for your rights and getting what you want regardless of other people. That is aggressive behaviour. One of the most central elements of assertive behaviour is appropriateness and respect for other people's feelings as well as your own. An assertive response should be appropriate:

◆ to you – so that you are not being false or plastic
◆ to the company – you are its representative
◆ to the customer – it is crucial to make the customer feel that you understand the particular problem.

Being assertive means being ready to cooperate with another person on an equal basis. It means being able to:

◆ address an issue calmly
◆ see a problem as there to be solved, without blaming yourself or other people
◆ be polite and courteous, without crawling
◆ be yourself and let other people be themselves
◆ make mistakes and learn from them
◆ be treated with respect, while respecting other people's rights
◆ deal with other people courteously without needing them to like you or what you are saying.

Service teams or companies that are successfully assertive become well known for their effective management of complaints. They savour complaints and don't shun them!

How can we make it easier?

Responding to complaints in an assertive and positive manner is the key. Individuals involved in service provision need to consider the difficult situations they most commonly face, and formulate assertive responses that will assist the complaint-handling process in reaching a better solution for customers and for the business.

Teams and individuals who deal with customers with complaints will find it useful to work through scenarios, analyse the way they currently respond and suggest more assertive responses, looking at the consequences of different responses. A format to facilitate the process might look like that in Table 6.2.

Table 6.2 *Complaints format*

Stage 1

You are faced with an angry customer. Record details of the complaint here:

Stage 2

The wrong response	*The right response*

I wasn't here at the time
There's nothing we can do
Perhaps you can sort it out
      yourself
You've come to the wrong
      department
etc.
	What could you say?

Stage 3

The consequences	*The consequences*

There are a few useful techniques that make it easier to deal with complaints.

Technique 1 – Solve the problem

Think of how to solve the problem rather than who is to blame. Even if you don't say so to the customer, you may find yourself thinking, 'That's not my job', 'That happened when I wasn't here' or 'I don't see why I should sort out somebody else's mess'. Sometimes it's easy to blame yourself when a situation goes wrong, thinking, 'I knew I should have...', 'I've made a real mess of this' or 'I can't get anything right'. Blaming either yourself or other people is a waste of time.

This is not to say that you can't recognize a mistake and learn from it, but that using your energy in trying to find out who is to blame merely makes you feel angry, resentful or sorry for yourself. It achieves nothing worthwhile. Dealing with customers' complaints invariably involves sorting out situations that are not directly your fault. The answer is to solve the problem and take it professionally, seeing it as just another part of the job.

Technique 2 – Find out what they want you to do

Listen carefully and repeat what the customer has said to check that you have understood and know what they want you to do. Often a customer will approach you with a complaint and with no suggestions for the solution. He or she might tell you exactly what is wrong. You will be told the whole story and why it caused such problems, but often you are left to suggest the solution yourself. You have apologized, listened sympathetically and shown that you understand.

Take a moment to think what you could do next.

You could ask more questions and listen carefully to their replies, to find out what they want you to do – if anything. Listening to the complaint is sometimes as important as doing something about it.

Technique 3 – Outline the solution or the alternatives

Handling an angry person with a complaint is quite simple when you can solve the problem. If you can, say so immediately. However, there may be occasions when you can't do exactly what they would like you to do. In such a situation, try to outline the alternatives or say what you can do.

Instead of saying, 'No, we can't do that,' what other words or phrases could you suggest as an alternative?

You could respond with phrases such as: 'It is possible to…', 'We do have…', 'I will check if…', 'I can (say what you can do) but I can't…', putting the positive before the negative.

Technique 4 – Take charge of the situation, say 'I will' and be positive

To give the customer more confidence in you, use 'I will' instead of 'I could', 'I might' or 'I don't', all of which sound weak and negative. For instance, instead of saying, 'I don't think we can do that, I could try to find out for you', say, 'I will go and find out for you'. Using 'will' sounds as if you are really doing something and therefore reassures the customer. 'I could try…' sounds vague and leaves the customer wondering if anything can or will be done.

To illustrate the difference, consider more positive-sounding alternatives to the following responses, which will demonstrate to the customer that something will be done.

1 'I'm not sure if the manager is back from lunch yet.'
   Positive phrase:

2   'I don't think we can do anything about that. I could find out for you, I suppose.'
Positive phrase:

_____

3   'I'm sorry you've had such a bad time. I'll try not to let it happen again.'
Positive phrase:

_____

Now have a look at the following possibilities and see how, from the customer's point of view, they constitute much more positive responses:

1 'I will see if the manager is available.'
2 'I will go and look in the stockroom for you.'
3 'I will see that this does not happen again.'

Technique 5 – Tell them what they can do, not what they can't

This is another technique where your response can be positive and active rather than negative and ineffective. Instead of saying 'No', say 'You can…'. It is much better from the customer's point of view to know what they can do rather than what they can't. This does not always work, as there isn't always an alternative. However, there are many situations where you can use this technique. You can use it:

◆ when you cannot give the customer exactly what they are asking for, but you have an alternative
◆ when you would like to help or show that you want to do so, but you are not able to do more than convey your goodwill

◆ when your customer does not know exactly what he or she wants. Giving customers an option often helps them make their mind up.

Even if you are not to blame for the problem, and you don't have control over the outcome, the best thing you can do is help solve the problem. Quite apart from giving your customer the best service you can and satisfying them as far as possible, it is better, from your own point of view, to be helpful. This is particularly true when you are having to deal with an angry or irritated person. Solving the problem as well as you can will help save time, reduce your stress levels and make you feel better, even if you cannot completely satisfy the customer.

It has to be said that being assertive doesn't always work. There may be occasions when it seems that all your good, assertive work has still failed and you feel you cannot win. For example, if you are dealing with an aggressive person who will not cooperate, or a passive person who insists on blaming themselves or trying to make you feel guilty, then you will probably not find a win/win solution. However, you will come out of the situation feeling that you have kept your self-respect and done your best. Remember:

◆ there are some people who will make it very difficult indeed for you to please them
◆ you are committed to providing your customer, whenever possible, with what he or she wants or needs.

Setting up a complaints system

So far in this chapter we have been considering the skills involved in dealing with customers face to face. This is crucial, but just as important is ensuring that a proper system is set up to collect, monitor and communicate complaints. The best systems incorporate the following features.

◆ A method exists for logging any complaint at the customer interface. Best are single-sheet formats incorporating information on action promised, when action will be taken, who is responsible for following it through, and suggestions on how to make sure it doesn't happen again.

◆ All logged complaints are sent to a central source.

◆ The central source records and classifies all complaints, looks for themes and produces an analysis by department, time of year or any other variable that might be pertinent to the organization.

◆ The complaints analysis is fed back to departments who are encouraged to evolve strategies to minimize the likelihood of these complaints arising again; these strategies are then fed back to the central source.

Beyond that, a key feature of any effective system must be that senior management are also given periodical reports that summarize the complaints and detail the strategies employed to remedy them. Developing staff skills and attitudes so that any customer complaint is dealt with speedily and effectively is essential, but so also is senior management's readiness to set up systems that enable the business to learn from what goes wrong. Therefore the process needs to ensure the following, in addition to the points already covered.

◆ All customer complaints are logged in a way that enables a picture to be built up of when errors occurred, the nature of each error, who was responsible, what was done to recover the situation and the level of satisfaction felt by the customer complaining (and, perhaps more importantly, his or her readiness to buy again).

◆ Seemingly satisfied customers are surveyed on a regular basis to ensure that there are no dissatisfactions that have not been conveyed.

◆ The 'big picture' of customer satisfaction, and levels and sources of complaint, are reviewed regularly by senior management and mechanisms are put in place to remedy problems and prevent recurrences.

◆ Problem-solving teams are formed from those who can most influence the improvements that need to be in place, and

their recommendations are implemented.
- ◆ A business-wide commitment is made to specific levels of reduction in customer complaints, and measurements are put in place to ensure that these targets are met.

Finally, whatever system used, it is vital to remind ourselves that the initial complaints must be dealt with immediately, at the customer interface. This involves giving front-liners considerable discretion, without their feeling that they have always to check with their managers. For example:

- ◆ the assistant at a fish and chip shop who can give you an extra piece of fish if you complain that your portion is too small
- ◆ the washing machine repair man who does not charge for part of the repair he has carried out because he believes that the part should not have broken, even though the guarantee has just run out
- ◆ the receptionist at a squash club who can offer a free game to an irate member who has been double booked.

Impressive recovery keeps customers loyal, makes staff feel good and motivated, and maintains a business's reputation.

Team/business questionnaire 9 – profiting from complaints

Excellent service businesses welcome complaints from customers, seeing them as opportunities to improve their service. They also know that a customer whose complaint is handled well is more likely to remain a customer than is one who is dissatisfied but cannot or does not complain. Quality service companies have a system for recording complaints and monitoring outcomes, and also invest in training their staff to deal with complaints.

You now have the opportunity to score your team or business on the way it profits from complaints (Table 6.3). The exercise is of most value if all your team members can complete the

Table 6.3 *Complaints questionnaire*

	Score
We are aware, as a business, that for every complaint received there could be 26 unhappy customers from whom we do not hear	☐
We know that an unhappy customer will on average tell 10 other people about the problem	☐
Complaints, although not pleasant, are welcomed. They are seen as second chances or moments of truth, providing another opportunity to impress the customer	☐
We make it easy for customers to complain	☐
Complaints are recorded, studied and learnt from	☐
The level and nature of complaints are reported at the most senior level	☐
We have effective recovery systems so that complaints are dealt with quickly and efficiently. The policy is to have a satisfied customer at the end of any problem or difficult situation	☐
We train people in the skills of effective complaint handling	☐
We empower front-liners to take fast, corrective action	☐
We know why we lose any customer	☐

The total possible score for profiting from complaints is 50

My score for profiting from complaints is   ☐

questionnaire, compare notes and plan action for continuous improvement.

Each statement should be scored in the following way:

Score 1: if you strongly disagree that the statement is true of your business.

Score 2: if you disagree that the statement is true of your business.

Score 3: if you see the statement as being somewhat true of your business.

Score 4: if you agree that the statement is true of your business.

Score 5: if you strongly agree that the statement is true of your business.

Three things that we could do to improve this score are:

_____

_____

Of these, the most important is:

_____

_____

7

IT'S CULTURE THAT COUNTS

A key purpose of this chapter is to provide an overview of the material covered in this book and to highlight and reinforce the most salient points. You have also had the opportunity to score your own team or organization on a number of aspects that are central to building a service business. In this chapter it is suggested that you transfer the results of those questionnaires on to a final summary, producing a broad picture of where your business is now in terms of customer focus. Then you are invited to develop an action plan addressing the key issues that stand out as a result of that analysis.

Over the last two decades, many companies have recommitted themselves to service as a key strategy for revitalizing their businesses. It is in the nature of a long corporate life that there are fluctuations, with better times and less good times. Frequently, when a business is felt to be flagging, when motivation seems lacking or divisions occur, there is a tendency to use a quality service programme to re-energize the corporate body.

Examples can be found of companies recommitting to service from any or all of the following standpoints:

◆ fear of falling behind the competition, where competitors have rejuvenated their approach to the customer and to service
◆ fear of being the division that will be disposed of when the group is downsizing
◆ the arrival of a new chief executive, or other senior director, who is passionate about service or is seeking to make his or her mark on the business
◆ a wish to develop a unifying philosophy to integrate businesses that have merged
◆ an indication from customer feedback of a real crisis of customer confidence

◆ a wasteful, damaging level of staff turnover as a result of low morale – people leaving because they feel that they are not trained or supported and that the company doesn't care

◆ ambition on the part of the company – although very satisfied with its business and reputation, it wants to be outstanding, to be 'world class' in its field

◆ a desire to change the corporate culture, from one that has been the basis for previous success to one that addresses a new age of customer awareness and service competition.

If your own company has renewed, or will shortly renew, its commitment to service excellence, what was, or will be, its business need?

Whatever the starting point, it is vital that such renewal is not seen, or approached, as a 'quick-fix' solution to a business problem. Many huge corporate budgets have been hurled at high-gloss, high-profile service programmes that have been comet-like in their impact – they burned bright and faded fast.

The most wasteful have been those programmes, known scathingly in the trade as 'smile training', in which the approach is simply to train front-liners in customer-contact skills (the 'have-a-nice-day' school of charm training). The impact of these programmes tends to be very short-lived and, frequently, a very damaging corporate belief that 'we have done customer service and it didn't work' is all that is left behind. This approach doesn't work because it fails to recognize two vital truths:

◆ Whether front-liners smile or not will be much more to do with how they are led and managed than with how they are trained.

◆ The challenge is not to get staff to smile at the customer, but to get the customer to smile at the staff because he or she has enjoyed the service experience.

So the realization is that any approach to establishing sustained, enhanced service cannot be simplistic and short term.

Features of a genuine service business

The approach to establishing a truly customer and service-oriented business has to be comprehensive, integrated, well resourced and well managed. It has to be seen as a 'total approach', comprising all of the following components.

A clear, motivating business mission or vision

High-quality service businesses recognize that all the varied and diverse efforts of those involved in the business need to be focused on a visible, challenging and inspiring common purpose.

If we don't know where we are going we could finish up somewhere else!

A great deal of attention is paid to communicating this common purpose – that is, the business mission or vision – so that it defines and drives departmental, team and individual perform-ance. The best missions are challenging but achievable, and cor-porate performance can be measured against them. They are motivating because they show people where their efforts fit in, they tell people 'what it's all for', 'where it's going', they give people something to aim for and something of which they can be proud. It is the job of leaders to define the mission, commu-nicate it relentlessly, plan its achievement and measure progress towards it.

One way of clarifying the mission is for the top team in the business to agree answers to the following questions:

◆ What is our corporate purpose and what are our priorities?
◆ What do we want our stakeholders (staff, customers, share-

holders and competitors) to say about our business and what do we want our reputation to be?

◆ Where do we want to be in two or three years' time?
◆ What will be our values as we build the business?
◆ What do we want our people to believe in, to be proud of, and what will they find inspiring as a purpose?

Visible and sustained commitment from the top

Business leaders must communicate and 'live' the vision of the service culture that they wish to create and the service ethic that they wish to establish. There must be one message from the top and every senior manager must be clear on the things that he or she can do, or not do, to model the service message. Tom Peters reminds the leaders of organizations that 'staff watch your feet, not your lips!'. If leaders are preaching service but practising something else – such as profit at any price – then people will believe the behaviour, not the words. Worse still, mixed messages dissipate energy and invite cynicism towards the leadership and towards corporate campaigns in general.

Any service quality programme must be led from the top. The top team have to be leaders, marketers and models of the service philosophy, and must realize the significance of their role. The leadership task is to provide, over a sustained period, vision, direction, values and philosophy, and to make clear what is non-negotiable (that is, commitment to the customer, to quality and to service). Beyond that, business leaders must provide support, encouragement, measurement of achievement, feedback on performance, recognition and reward, scope for drive, ownership and initiative and, above all, consistent direction over years.

Ownership by line managers

Line managers will make or break any programme of culture change. Getting their commitment and making them leaders and owners of the initiative are prerequisites for success. It is said that 85 per cent of what happens in companies is down to managers, so they must be given the right tools to establish the quality and service priority. Managing in a quality service business requires specialist skills.

'Hearts and minds' commitment from front-liners

The customer's experience is created by front-liners. Unless they have the necessary confidence, motivation and skills, unless they feel enthused and empowered to put the customer first and unless they feel respected and well managed, then customers will not feel any difference from the competition. The 'hearts and minds' approach recognizes that quality and service require a combination of passion and enthusiasm, together with systematic, structured application, to achieve long-term results.

Quality training and development

Training design, delivery and materials must stimulate interest and be intrinsically motivating, relevant, work based and customized to the business style and culture. They must be practical in that they equip managers and front-liners with the tools to do the job. To achieve the ownership that is key to success in service-enhancement programmes, there should be no perception of 'off-the-shelf' programmes being introduced by outsiders. The corporate experience must be that 'we have grown our own programme'. Quality and service must be owned by the whole company; it must not belong to any one executive, department or function, or be seen as an aside to the mainstream business activity. Commitment to quality and service is not optional, it is the *raison d'être* of every job and every business function.

Any initiative must be more than simply a training programme, in which the tendency can be to produce an adjunct to the mainstream business. It must link the training and development of people to the mission and show them their part in realizing it. It must link quality and service to performance management, to accountability and to the bottom line.

Progressive businesses recognize clearly that their people are their greatest asset. It is difficult to stay ahead of the competition simply in product terms – products are easily and quickly copied. Staying impressive to customers, locking them into a business and keeping them loyal to it over years, is likely to be achievable only through the quality, motivation and commitment of the people in the business. Quality performance from talented people is essential for differentiation and business success. Investing in their development is essential if a business is to grow, and if the deliverers are to be motivated and attracted to stay to achieve the mission. There is a need to be clear about what competencies the business will need, and for a development programme that delivers those competencies to its people.

A clear understanding of the competencies needed at each level to build the business and deliver the mission

Progressive businesses are now able to describe competency profiles (the skills, qualities and attitudes required) at each level and in each area of the organization. They are able to say, 'These are the most effective senior managers, this is what they believe and do that makes them the most effective, and this is what we require in our senior managers now and at the next stage of our development'. These businesses will have the same ability to describe competency profiles for middle managers and front-liners.

Recruitment, induction and advancement

The best businesses are clear about the talent and competencies that they need to attract. Recruitment is a quality process, focusing on the skills and qualities required. Those selected are given a quality induction into the business, which provides them with the information they need, clearly establishes for them where the business is going, what will be expected of them and what they can expect in return. The best businesses also 'grow their own' leaders, developing the next generation of senior managers from the best of their talent.

Data and research

A company committed to quality service must use research to learn from the customer externally, and the staff internally, about perceptions of quality and areas for improvement. It must use the data that the research produces to shape policy, to educate staff and to drive performance in the business.

One world-famous retail business has now established the links between staff morale, customer satisfaction and profitability. From management work to enhance the positive attitudes to the business among the staff, it is able to measure percentage increases in morale. Within a given period, it is then able to trace percentage increases in customer satisfaction and, most interestingly, in sales and profits. By learning from its staff what it would take to make the organization a compelling place to work, by training the business leaders to demonstrate a high level of interpersonal skills, integrity, service orientation and the ability and readiness to empower staff, the organization has seen a parallel increase in staff morale, customer satisfaction and profitability.

Measuring and appraising performance

The most effective organizations are able to be specific about the performance that they require of individuals in pursuit of business success. They set objectives and appraise performance against these. They equip their managers to carry out regular, constructive and motivating appraisal sessions.

Consciousness of the bottom line

The business case for investment in service enhancement has been clearly established and is summed up in the phrase 'customer retention'. The research on customer behaviour is unequivocal, and some key customer service statistics from all business sectors support the commercial case for a recommitment to service quality. Various research projects indicate that:

◆ increasing customer retention by as little as 5 per cent can raise profits by 25 to 30 per cent
◆ cutting defection rates to 5 per cent can increase net value for each customer by 75 per cent
◆ service companies often lose between 10 and 18 per cent of their customers annually
◆ in some service companies, up to 35 per cent of staff can be involved in correcting errors
◆ organizations with concise, understandable and actionable service strategies, and a powerful service vision, are four times as likely to receive superior service ratings from their customers than are those without them

◆ in organizations where employees understand their roles in the service delivery process, customer satisfaction rates are double those in organizations where customer-focused roles and activities have not been defined (76 as against 35 per cent)

◆ in companies that share customer evaluations with front-liners and support staff, customer satisfaction ratings jump from 50 to 81 per cent

◆ customer satisfaction ratings double when organizations set standards for responding to customer complaints or questions, and for minimizing customers' waiting time

◆ in organizations with a customer-retention strategy, 56 per cent of employees said that their managers spend time talking and listening to customers, compared with 28 per cent in organizations with no such policy

◆ customers who have complaints solved on first contact with customer service representatives are more interested in being cross-sold other products.

Common ground can therefore now be established between those who believe in service *per se*, convinced that investing in its enhancement is simply the best way to run a business, and those finance specialists who may not subscribe solidly to the philosophy without proof that the investment will bring returns. But if it is to bring forth its real fruits, the commitment to continuous service improvement must be sustained.

The US Government's General Audit Office examined the benefits that accrued to corporations that made applications to be considered for the prestigious Baldrige Award (a national award for corporate performance in quality). It found that it could take up to three years for companies to see any return on the investment made in quality and service programmes.

Obsession with the customer
Tom Peters observed that his many years' experience of deep involvement in organizations showed clearly that:

Businesses that make profit their priority are never as profitable as those that make quality and service to their customer the priority!

Commitment to the customer and to service quality (real commitment, not lip service or mixed messages) is a hallmark of top businesses. They recognize that 'the customer is boss', and without the customer there can be no jobs, salaries, profits, bonuses or dividends. These businesses organize, communicate, train, develop, measure and reward in support of this priority.

Systems

The most successful businesses are clear that, in pursuit of the quality of service that they wish to deliver to their customers, they must establish efficient, effective business systems, backed by appropriate technology, that provide customers with what they want, when they want it. They have equally effective systems to support quality performance and information needs, in-house.

Communication

Top businesses are committed to quality communication with their people. In various ways, they keep the mission and priorities very visible, they communicate progress and achievements, they build up a message of momentum and achievement, and they educate their people about the business, its standing, its competition, and about their key role in building success.

Leadership

Quality businesses have quality leaders, who provide a clear vision of where the business is going, what it will take to be successful, and provide energy, enthusiasm, support, encouragement and recognition. From the top team, there is the same message, nobody 'sings from a different hymn sheet', there is no evidence of 'a house divided' and no mixed messages to staff. Top team members have 'the picture on the lid of the jigsaw', in that they can see, and explain to others, how all pieces, activities and enterprises in the business fit together. Other people can see the pieces, but leaders let them understand the whole. Quality leaders are visible to their people and make them feel valued and appreciated.

Worthy of external recognition

Recognition for achievement is a powerful motivator, at the corporate as well as the individual level. Many companies are focusing on the European Quality Award (EQA) as a means of getting future recognition for their commitment to, and achievement in, quality. and service. They are using its criteria as benchmarks for their own work and will eventually make submissions for an award against these. They believe that the EQA criteria – which require high performance in the areas of leadership, people management, policy and strategy, resources, processes, people satisfaction, customer satisfaction, impact on society and business results – are not only a most useful template for assessing corporate quality, but also represent an excellent model for seeking external recognition for corporate achievement. The EQA is emulating the impact of the Baldrige Award in the USA, and will surely become the goal for all ambitious companies operating in Europe and internationally.

A service culture

Each business develops its own culture and, in the end, it is culture that influences long-term behaviour in organizations. Culture is a powerful but seemingly mystical concept. In fact, it is a very observable, recognizable pattern of life in an organization, which influences the behaviour of those who work in it.

An observer can easiily distinguish features of the particular culture in major organizations such as British Airways or Virgin, in ICI or Marks & Spencer, in the major banks or IT companies, in the Civil Service, in national or local government, in the armed forces and so on. Those bodies have asked themselves, 'What kind of organization do we want, or need, to be? What kind of culture do we need to be successful?' They have then created their cultures consciously – and, to an extent, unconsciously – to achieve their success. These cultures are, of course, non-transferable. For instance, it is difficult to imagine a bank's culture being applied to running an airline, or a Civil Service culture applied to running an IT business.

In their long lives, companies sometimes have to reshape their cultures to meet new business circumstances. Many traditional building societies, with their mutual histories, have had to undergo significant culture changes to meet new commercial challenges, and that has been a painful experience for many of those who have spent their working lives in unchanging organizations. It is not only financial services that have had to adapt to meet the demands of new, fast-changing global markets. Ask British Airways staff how that culture was changed when Lord King and Colin Marshall renewed the ailing airline; ask ICI staff who worked with John Harvey-Jones how he reshaped that business and how its culture changed to bring it new success.

Culture is created, and re-created, by recognizing and acting on the factors that shape it. It is the product of the following.

◆ *History and tradition* – what has worked in the past, who the heroes and heroines are, the legends about them, what has to be respected, how 'things are done around here', what is approved of and what is frowned on.
◆ *Corporate values* – the values that drive and shape the organization.
◆ *Rules and regulations* – what authority requires of people, what it insists on, what is dictated, what the givens are, and where people are free to choose.
◆ *Leadership* – who the leaders are, what they did to get where they are, how they relate to and treat people, their style of leadership, and what they preach as priorities.
◆ *Measurement* – what is measured in the business (what you measure is what you get!) and the performance criteria used for appraisal.
◆ *Training* – the specific themes and messages that are focused on in development programmes, what is emphasized and what are recurrent themes.
◆ *Reward and recognition* – (what you measure and reward is what you really get!), the patterns of reward and recognition, and the messages about 'what really matters round here'.

Creating a service culture is a major task. It cannot be done by simply talking about it, writing about it, producing training programmes to encourage it, or expecting it to happen overnight. It is not easy to achieve, but no company will be a significant player unless it creates a service culture and ethic, because it will be the culture that, in the long term, shapes the behaviour of its people.

The organization's leadership has to be clear about:

◆ the features of the culture that are required in the business to achieve its mission
◆ the values and behaviour that it wants to be most evident
◆ how the present culture is described and its predominant features and influences
◆ how, in two or three years' time, it wants people to describe what it is like to work in the company, what matters most, what the business expects of them, and what they have to do, and be, to get on there.

Years of experience of working with major companies in the field of quality and service suggests that successful programmes involve fundamental culture change, embedding the quality and service ethos, and a belief in continuous improvement, deep in the working life of everybody in the business. This is achieved only through sustained attention to all these various areas of corporate activity. There are no short-cuts to creating a quality, customer-driven culture, and to the success that this brings.

Team/business questionnaire 10 – a culture to support your mission

Each business develops its own culture and, in the end, it is culture that is the long-term influencer and shaper of behaviour in organizations. You now have the opportunity to score your team or business on its service culture (Table 7.1). As before, this type of exercise is of most value if all your team members can complete the questionnaire, compare notes and plan action for continuous improvement.

Table 7.1 *Culture questionnaire*

	Score
We have a clearly identified organizational culture that supports our mission	[ ]
Our people are clear on our values and priorities, and these are recognized as consistent with our business purpose and important to our success	[ ]
Our top team members 'walk the talk'. They promote the culture and senior and middle managers are seen as united in support of it. They live the values and there are no mixed messages about what the business needs to be successful	[ ]
We are clear about the competencies and qualities that individuals need to be successful in our culture and to make our business successful	[ ]
We recruit the kind of people who will 'fit' our culture; you get on here by doing things 'our way'	[ ]
Our training and development programmes enhance the competencies and values that we need to grow and maintain business success	[ ]
There is a strong sense of ownership of and pride in our culture, together with allegiance to it among line managers and front-liners	[ ]
There is a strong sense of ownership in and pride in our culture and allegiance to it across all areas of the business	[ ]
Our culure is one that will enable us to achieve our business ambitions for the next two to three years. There are no changes required	[ ]

The total possible score for a culture to support our mission is 50

My score for a culture to support our mission is   [ ]

Each statement should be scored in the following way:

Score 1: if you strongly disagree that the statement is true of your business.

Score 2: if you disagree that the statement is true of your business.

Score 3: if you see the statement as being somewhat true of your business.

Score 4: if you agree that the statement is true of your business.

Score 5: if you strongly agree that the statement is true of your business.

Three things that we could do to improve this score are:

_____

_____

_____

Of these, the most important is:

_____

_____

In summary

It is hoped that the material in this final chapter has gone some way towards condensing and summarizing many of the key concepts and much of the learning to be found throughout the book. As you have worked with the material, you have had the opportunity to use 10 questionnaires to rate, with your team, where you perceive your business to be in terms of those factors that are central to service excellence.

Over a period of time, it may be interesting to measure your business's achievements in addressing any shortcomings, by revisiting the questionnaires.

You might wish now to transfer the results from each of the questionnaires to the tally sheet in Table 7.2 to produce an

Table 7.2 *Final summary*

Chapter	Questionnaire	Score
2	1 Service management	

Three things that we could do to improve this score:

Of these, the most important is:

| 2 | 2 Your mission or vision | |

Three things that we could do to improve this score:

Of these, the most important is:

| 3 | 3 Focus on your customer | |

Three things that we could do to improve this score:

Of these, the most important is:

| 3 | 4 Internal service quality | |

Three things that we could do to improve this score:

Of these, the most important is:

| 4 | 5 Moments of truth | |

Three things that we could do to improve this score:

Of these, the most important is:

Table 7.2 *Final summary (cont.)*

Chapter	Questionnaire	Score
4	6 The 4 Ps	☐

Three things that we could do to improve this score:

Of these, the most important is:

5	7 Quality service standards	☐

Three things that we could do to improve this score:

Of these, the most important is:

5	8 Measurement	☐

Three things that we could do to improve this score:

Of these, the most important is:

6	9 Profiting from complaints	☐

Three things that we could do to improve this score:

Of these, the most important is:

7	10 A culture to support your mission	☐

Three things that we could do to improve this score:

Of these, the most important is:

Table 7.2 *Final summary (cont.)*

Our final overall score (maximum possible = 500) ☐

Our two strongest areas appear to be:

The two areas needing most work appear to be:

---

overview, and perhaps highlight the broad areas in which your business possesses strengths and those in which developmental work is probably required.

Of course, this is not an entirely scientific analysis of your business's standing in the eyes of its customers, because it is the result of collating the opinions of people working in the business, and opinions, by their very nature, are subjective. However, the benefit of the exercise is that it does help identify areas for development and is a starting point for formulating action plans.

Setting objectives and forming action plans

In the summary chart, you can record the areas for action that were identified as you completed the questionnaires. You may wish to review these findings and, with your team, develop an overall action plan for beginning to work on those areas where, at the outset, you are likely to achieve success and, at the same time, make an impact on the quality of service that your customers experience. Having re-examined what you have discovered from completing the questionnaires, decide, as a team, which areas those are. For each broad area in which you initially decide to work for improvements, set yourselves a few clear objectives.

For example:

To improve our internal service quality, we will:

1
2
3

Then decide how you will build on each objective and convert it into an action plan.

For example:

To achieve Objective 1, we will:

1
2
3

To achieve Objective 2, we will:

1
2
3

and so on.

Then consider how you will know when you have achieved each objective.

For example:

We will review progress on: (date) . . . .

And again on: (date). . . . .

Put dates for these reviews in your diary.

As you work through this objective-setting and action-planning process, it is vital to bear in mind that the aim is not unwavering adherence to an original plan that has been set in concrete. Objectives and plans are there to be revised in the light of experience and new learning, and it is valuable to set time aside, perhaps on a monthly basis, for the specific purpose of discussing progress and reviewing your plans.

Finally, we very much hope that you have enjoyed the material in this book, and that you will be able to apply your learning to build a service business and bring about real benefits for yourself, your team and, of course, your customers, as you continue on the journey towards new and better standards of service in this service age!

INDEX

50 Training Activities for Administrative, Secretarial and Support Staff

Elizabeth Sansom and Christine Newton

An organization is only as good as its support staff, the
unsung heroes and heroines who keep the system going.
It is their competence and commitment that spell the
difference between disaster and triumph. Yet very little
material has been available to meet their particular
training needs.

This collection fills that gap. It is a comprehensive and
carefully structured collection of training sessions intended to
improve performance and motivation across a wide range of
topics. Each activity is fully participative and designed to
stimulate creativity, encourage empowerment and make
learning enjoyable. Topics covered range from induction for
the new recruit, through core concerns like customer care,
telephone skills and written communication, to tasks for the
more experienced such as project management and
presentation. There are projects, roleplays, games, case
studies, pencil-and-paper exercises, discussions - the whole
gamut of learning processes.

This is a manual that can be recommended with confidence
to any trainer, supervisor or team leader keen to strengthen
support staff skills.

Gower

10 Teambuilders
Ready-to-run Games for Team Development

Michèle Barca and Kate Cobb

The toughest obstacle you face when developing people is
often the people themselves - or rather their mindset.
10 Teambuilders is a collection that allows you to challenge
the imagination of your participants to leave their old mental
constraints behind them. Each of the games places your
people in situations and environments that are very different
from those with which they are familiar; they're astronauts on
a mission to Saturn; members of an archaeological team; or
part of a specialist bomb-disposal team.

To make sure that you not only engage your people's
enthusiasm and sense of fun, but that you also achieve a
significant learning outcome, Michèle Barca and Kate Cobb
include plenty of guidance to help you plan, run and debrief
each of the games. There are also background notes, models
and techniques on the five key areas, which you can develop
into handouts or presentations to support your session.
The running time on the 10 games varies between 45 and 90
minutes, making them suitable for both residential courses
and half-day team development sessions.

Gower

Sales Training

Frank Salisbury

Sales Training is widely recognized as the standard reference for trainers on all aspects in the development of sales people. This new edition, now published by Gower, takes the reader through the step-by-step process of training as it relates specifically to sales. Frank Salisbury explains the role of sales people, the skills they require and the best approach to take in training them. The author introduces new material on structured and professional selling, the use of non-verbal language training, techniques for sales managers to develop staff in the field, and the role of motivation. A whole new focus is that of developing sales managers as coaches and the crucial impact this can have on sales people and thus a company's success. Frank Salisbury advocates that selling should be seen as a physical skill, which can be learned by everyone. This pragmatic approach underpins Sales Training, making it an essential guide for any organization which wants to take the development of professional sales people seriously.

Gower